FURNITURE STUDIO 5

The Meaning of Craft

detail of *Accoutrements from the Planet Zoron* (2006)
Brad Johns
San Diego State University, CA
from *Faculty Selects 2006*, p. 108

FURNITURE STUDIO 5

The Meaning of Craft

Annual journal of The Furniture Society

The Furniture Society
Asheville, NC

The Furniture Society is a non-profit organization whose mission is to advance the art of furniture making by inspiring creativity, promoting excellence, and fostering understanding of this art and its place in society.

Furniture Studio 5
The Meaning of Craft
ISBN 10: 0967100445
ISBN 13: 9780967100449
Copyright ©2007 by The Furniture Society
All rights reserved

Editor: John Kelsey
Design and layout: Maura J. Zimmer
Copy editor: Kate Garrenson

Printed in the United States of America on FSC-certified paper containing 10% post-consumer recycled waste
First printing: August 2007

Library of Congress Cataloging-in-Publication Data

The meaning of craft : Furniture Studio 5 / edited by John Kelsey.
    p. cm. -- (Furniture Studio ; 5)
 Includes index.
 ISBN 978-0-9671004-4-9
 1. Furniture--United States--History--21st century. I. Kelsey, John, 1946-
 NK2408.2.M43 2007
 749.0973--dc22

                                 2007025683

THE FURNITURE SOCIETY
111 Grovewood Road
Asheville, NC 28804
Phone: 828-255-1949; fax 828-255-1950
www.furnituresociety.org

Preface

Volume 5 of the *Furniture Studio* series represents a milestone in many ways. The Windgate Charitable Foundation gave The Furniture Society a grant to resume publication of our series in 2004. As a result, and with the able leadership of John Kelsey, we have published three volumes of thoughtful and provocative writing showcasing the most important and current works in studio furniture. Volume 5, *The Meaning of Craft*, represents the best of this experience and illustrates to our membership and the general public just how vibrant the art and craft of furniture making has become. These three volumes owe much to the Windgate Charitable Foundation and on behalf of the Society, I'd like to express our great appreciation.

This volume is also significant to me in that we are publishing the writings of some of our younger and brighter makers. Please pay special attention to the Manifesto story on page 8, as it embodies the future of the studio furniture world as well as offering insights on the craft world in general. I am so pleased to be able to publish these thoughts and to highlight these members in a way that makes their thoughts available to you, our reader. Society President Gabriel Romeu has worked diligently to bring these manifestoes to you in a way that is accessible while retaining the original meaning. They were written for a presentation at our 2006 conference and have become a topic of discussion far beyond the Society's virtual walls.

This publishing project now enters a hiatus, while the society's trustees evaluate the work and its impact, and consider how to proceed.

—*Andrew H. Glasgow, Executive Director, The Furniture Society*

Foreword

The *Furniture Studio* publishing project originated in a beery late-night conversation during the first Furniture Society conference, held in 1997 at the State University of New York in Purchase. In December of that year I made a formal proposal to the Society board of trustees, Rick Mastelli joined the project as co-editor, and together with art director Deborah Fillion we produced *The Heart of the Functional Arts* (1999). In 2000 and 2001 we three again collaborated to create the second volume, *Tradition in Contemporary Furniture*. These two books were supported by a generous grant from an anonymous foundation.

Furniture Studio then went on hold until 2004 when a new grant enabled the Society to embark upon the current three-volume series. I was again hired as editor, along with art director Maura J. Zimmer. Working very closely with the Society's Editorial Advisory Board, we published Vol. 3, *Furniture Makers Exploring Digital Technologies* (2005), Vol. 4, *Focus on Materials* (2006), and the book you now hold, Vol. 5, *The Meaning of Craft* (2007).

I have been writing, editing, and publishing about woodworking and furniture making since 1974. I'll just conclude by saying that the *Furniture Studio* project has been the most interesting and challenging of my career. I'm deeply grateful to The Furniture Society for granting me these opportunities, as I remain awestruck by the boundless creativity of our working furniture makers.

—*John Kelsey, Editor,* Furniture Studio

Mission

Furniture Studio, the annual journal of The Furniture Society, presents images and ideas about studio furniture, furniture making and design, and furniture makers/artists. By placing studio furniture in an artistic, social, cultural, and historical context, the journal promotes a better understanding of the work and inspires continuing advancement in the art of furniture making.

Policy

It is the editorial policy of *Furniture Studio* to represent all aspects of the studio furniture field, reflecting its diversity as to age, gender, materials, and stylistic preference. A broad range of connoisseurs, writers, critics, and historians from within and outside the field offers reflection and opinion in the journal. The journal encourages the work of emerging designers, makers, and writers.

Mission and policy statement adopted by The Furniture Society Editorial Advisory Board, May 2004

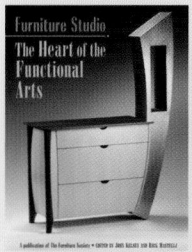
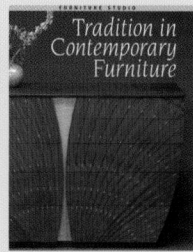
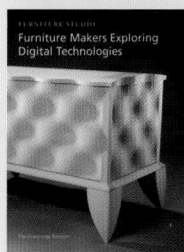

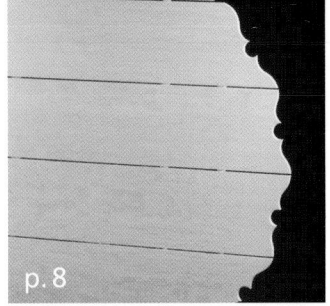

p. 8

p. 20

p. 30

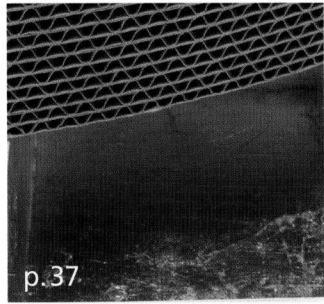

p. 37

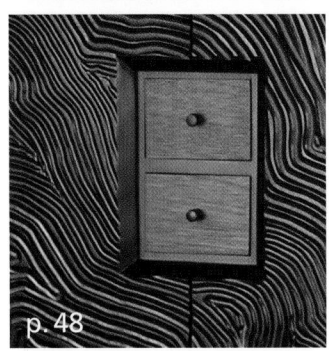

p. 48

p. 58

Contents

p. 66

p. 81

p. 96

p. 110

p. 122

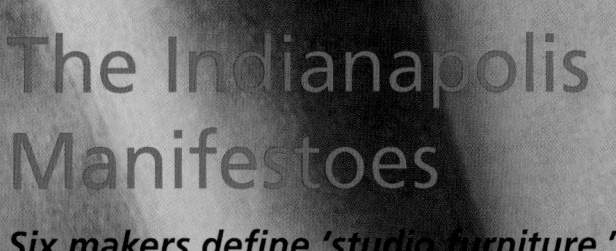

The Indianapolis Manifestoes

*Six makers define 'studio furniture,'
and what it means to make it*

Introduction by Gabriel Romeu

Jennifer Anderson
detail of *Conversation*, p. 14

The Furniture Society's 2006 conference in Indianapolis gave six emerging educators and makers a forum for their thoughts on the present and future of the studio furniture field. The six prepared essays that were collected and published as a small booklet under the title *M06: Manifestoes for the Next Generation*, which they presented through the format of the Critical Discourse panel. The project was organized and moderated by Tom Loeser, who heads the dynamic furniture program at the University of Wisconsin (Madison).

The manifesto discussions stirred a conversation that was both lively and heated. I spent quite a lot of time re-reading the manifestoes and grappling with the issues they presented, looking for a way to summarize the discussion for this journal. I made a lot of scrap paper, without much progress toward my goal. But then, a few months after our Indianapolis conference, I attended the American Craft Council symposium in Houston, entitled "The Future of Craft" (see page 30). I imagined that the symposium would divert me from my struggle with the manifestoes, but instead it gave me the revelation that these writers were already clued in to, and aligned with, the larger conversation about the future of craft: that the issues confronting makers of studio furniture also confront every maker across the craft world.

I concluded that the best way to summarize the Indianapolis manifestoes was to extract a brief but telling excerpt from each (see pages 10 to 19), and to present it alongside images of the author's recent work. I thought you would see what they were getting at in their work, and if you wanted to learn more about the views of each writer, you could download a PDF of their complete texts (see box).

A few questions

And I was left with a list of questions to ponder, which I'll share with you below.

Furniture, of all categories of things, is finally made whole by the interaction of object to the body. Use and function consummates its identity. Is a furniture piece more successful when function is an inherent quality rather than an inferred reference, that is, when it is a "hyper-object?"

With the exposition of ideas and ironies having had prominence in the studio furniture field, especially in the gallery and museum, is there still a place for domestic problem-solving in the conception and implementation of a furniture piece? If there is, is it possible to talk about problem-solving functional furniture as seriously as we discuss less functional art objects that have a natural affinity to text-based analysis?

Gabriel Romeu is president of The Furniture Society.

Artspeak

Hybrid object: *"Hybrid" meaning of mixed origin or composition; an object that comes from more than one tradition or discourse, such as furniture/ sculpture, gas/electric, craft/conceptual art/video/ installation. Tommy Simpson, page 110, hybridizes furniture, sculpture, painting, and storytelling.*

Hyper object: *"Hyper" meaning above, beyond; sometimes connoting excess or exaggeration, a hyper object "means" more than ordinary objects; Marcel Duchamp's* Fountain *(his signed urinal), for example, or Garry Bennett's* Nail Cabinet.

—*defined by David Richardson.*
  Richardson writes for the After Hours blog at www.furnituresociety.org.

Hybrid objects *combine two or more objects, creating a new and perhaps bewildering situation. "Hybrid" is rooted in the Dadaists and the Surrealist painter René Magritte.*

Hyper objects *go beyond regular reality and become more than real. "Hyper" is rooted in pop art. Wendell Castle's* Table with Gloves and Keys *is a hyper object—looks real but cannot be used.*

The power of art illuminates the essence of subject, object, and the mystery of life; the hybrid by juxtaposition of two situations, and the hyper through enhancing the familiar. Many objects will not fit neatly into one or the other.

—*defined by Stephen Hogbin, whose work appears on page 84. In June 2007 Hogbin was given the first Professional Outreach Program Merit Award by the American Association of Woodturners.*

The nature of a commission requires the maker to sublimate the ego of self-expression to accommodate the needs of the Other. When success and prestige are determined by wealth and power, and self-indulgence is glorified, could it be subversive to cater with humility and technical mastery to the well-being of the Other? Is it perhaps a greater benefit to utilize craft/technical expertise to design for a mass market rather than for the indulgences of an individual? Can the commission process enhance self-expression instead of sublimating it? Can the commission be seen as an extension of the collaboration?

Can studio furniture provide a critique and alternative to the mass market of poorly produced furnishings? Can studio furniture provide a critique and alternative to the well-made designer alternatives?

Is it possible for studio furniture to educate and promote environmental sustainability? Small production models in support of a local economy? Individual expression rather than condescension to the collective?

Is traditional making as contemporary an approach as any other, except that the choices made refer to an earlier history? Are invention and creativity just adaptation?

Can some of the Utopian ideals that were prevalent in the 19th and 20th centuries have relevance on a smaller and more personal scale today?

Does the studio furniture object gain additional meaning and provenance with age, compared to the production object? Does studio furniture add to the notion of "heirloom?"

To download an illustrated PDF of the complete Indianapolis manifestoes, please visit:

http://www.furnituresociety.org/confer/furn26/manifesto2006.pdf.

Studio Furniture in the Expanded Field
Matthew Hebert, Chicago, IL

Art is an activity consisting in producing relationships with the world with the help of signs, forms, actions and objects.

—Nicolas Bourriaud, *Relational Aesthetics*, les presses du reel, 1998.

Where does studio furniture belong? According to the above definition, studio furniture falls squarely into the world of art practice. A studio furniture object meets the criteria in spades. What type of object could better modulate the viewer's relationship with the world than studio furniture?

Matthew Hebert
Dynamo Rocker (2005)
Repurposed school desk, oak, and electronics
16" x 24" x 40"

Fidgeting or rocking in the chair activates an electrical dynamo, which powers the lamp. —*MH*

Matthew Hebert
Seismo Table (2001)
Plywood, glass, electronics, and paper
36" x 20" x 16"

The apparatus visible beneath the glass records vibrations ranging from people walking to earthquakes, as well as any static electrical charges carried by individuals, and traces their amplitude onto a roll of paper, which spills out into the room. —*MH*

Convincing the rest of the art world to accept studio furniture with open arms now becomes the problem. In order to enter into dialogue with the contemporary world of art, it is important to understand its concerns. While the studio furniture world has a history of introspection and critical discourse, it is a needle in the haystack of art theory; art theory had a bit of a head start.

From my experience, defining our work through negation is prevalent within the studio furniture community. Common instances include: not-sculpture/not-design, not-sculpture/not-craft, not-design/not-art, not-art/not-craft, or maybe not-design/not-craft, etc. In conversation these terms are usually put into a structure such as: "Studio furniture is somewhere between x and y," where x and y are any two of the above pairs. The problem I have with all of these definitions is that they rely on verbs and not nouns. Almost anything can

be seen as the product of some amount of art, craft, and design.

I believe that studio furniture refers to the work of furniture makers operating in an art mode of production. To put studio furniture into a system between the negatives of these two terms is to suggest that it resides in a realm between architecture, spaces, and shelters on one side, and discrete functional objects on the other. A studio is quite different from a shop, not to mention a factory. The word "studio" conjures up images of the painter painting over his canvas or the sculptor trying to capture his muse in stone. Studio furniture makers create work to be sold through galleries or commissions; this model of distribution extends this comparison with other studio artists further. I suggest that studio furniture, due to the nature of its creation and production, is something different from furniture design and historic furniture reproduction work.

If we, the studio furniture community, broadened the definition of ourselves through the adoption

Matthew Hebert
Echo Table (2001)
Plywood, glass, electronics, and fabric
36" x 36" x 12"

The apparatus visible beneath the glass records sounds and conversation on a loop of tape, then replays the sounds after a 20-second delay. It has the effects of generating a reflective experience for the solitary viewer, or of making conversation nearly impossible for a group. —*MH*

of a more inclusive definition, we could open up a lot of new avenues with our work. We could fulfill the promise of studio furniture, which is to be a field of artistic creation connected to the greater art world. The artists creating work in this expanded field of studio furniture are rigorously examining what it means to create functional and aesthetic objects in our present day, and how these objects set up relationships between people and space.

Making New: Use, Image, and Action
Vivian Beer, Penland, NC

In this manifesto new is the most important adjective. I'm interested in making things that are new rather than modern.

The tension between image, the sampling of a metaphorical or referential "look" of a thing, and use, which is an active in-the-moment process of experience, is the key to our new making. I am interested in objects that are pulled on a spectrum between ergonomics and image, play and use, intimacy and performance.

Studio furniture occupies a social niche between the artist's studio, the craftsman's intimate knowledge of materials, and the designer's goal to provide, augment, and subtly brainwash the public with functional items. It follows a handmade tradition and this is very important, not simply because of

Vivian Beer
Scion (2004)
Fabricated sheet and bar stock steel
25" H x 23" W x 26.5" D

Thinking of a chair as a drawing I wanted to contrast the curves with rectangles. The weight of the line and nature of its curve, when translated into material, take on the tactile relationships of springiness and stiffness. When translated further into a relationship of use these qualities create the tactile sensation of sitting on a metal pillow. —VB

Vivian Beer
Winded Orange (2006)
Steel, paint
22" H x 24" W x 74" D

Covered in a Mazda car's color this bench is a conglomeration of familiar images. An out of breath orange bench made from memories of a bike's banana seat and mares' tails in the sky when weather is about to change. —VB

Vivian Beer
Filled with Birds and Beasts (2004)
Steel, paint
36" W x 54" H x 92" D

Sampling images that represent animals and forces in nature packs a piece with metaphor. The goal, however, is not to simply create something referential but a new thing—a hybrid object with a life of its own. —*VB*

the style or elegance of a hand-cut dovetail, not for the thoughtful practice of mastery, nor even the rich history of desire through decorative form. It is important because it provides the autonomy of the artist studio—of the small scale or small-scale production. Therefore its practitioners can afford to risk much more in service of their artistic voice. The lower the overhead the larger the steps one author can take. Our shops have autonomy from mass-marketing, mass-production systems. We live an intimate experimental experience of material with the power of function as a subject or script for our objects' lives in the world. The responsibility of this niche is to push the boundaries of meaning in utilitarian objects, to be a brand new, brand-free, bitch session made into things. I believe in the art we can touch, live with, sit on, or step in. I believe the form these objects take are questions holding curiosity, both echoing and creating our ideals.

I'm not really interested in why we live with furniture but rather how it can affect us. The devil and angel is in the details, and any theology at work

Vivian Beer
Red-Letter (2003) in use
Wood, paint, steel mechanism
29" H x 17" W x 30" D

A chair about balance and play just had to be red. —*VB*

will appear, like evidence in court, through the description. Critical looking, seeing, and talking at its best is a tool to dive deeper into our world and the objects we make. An action of design can be questioned, answered, or changed.

How much time do we spend paying the bills instead of thinking/seeing the world around us—the world we are supporting and creating? We are a force of nature—this is both terrifying and encouraging. What we see and how we see, our desire is our source. The autonomy of our studios and the objects we make within them is our power.

The question of how is harder than why, with why; we can float into a space of distanced meaning rather than chipping at the mundane, concrete, and complicated now. Use this studio, these hands and these skills to dive deep. Make a new thing. Find a rudder. Making new things requires us to look at the nature of what we are doing long enough to see it. Seeing is the hardest thing in the world; it has nothing to do with our eyes and everything to do with now.

Vivian Beer's piece Current *is shown on the cover.*

The Future of Studio Furniture
Jennifer Anderson, San Diego, CA

I live in the 21st century and I am a maker of one-of-a-kind objects; I am an artist, I am a craftsperson, I am a designer.

While studio furniture making has been traditionally tied to the field of craft, I believe its future belongs squarely at the intersection of art, craft, and design. If studio furniture making and craft are to survive, they must evolve. We must get past the belief that change is a terrible thing, and realize that humankind's progress and advances can help us with our work. Variations and diversity make every object unique and interesting, but our human hand doesn't need to touch something at every stage of the process in order to make it unique.

Jennifer Anderson
Conversation (male and female chairs) (2006)
Stainless steel, leather, and fiberglass; 30" H x 20 W x 19" D (each chair)

I don't pretend to have an answer to the fate of the field of studio furniture making and the world of craft. I share that dream of living and working in a little shop tucked away in some idyllic coastal village, where I will grow old making things with my hands. The only difference is that I will continue to challenge the boundaries of my work. I will not be restricted by the constraints of tradition; rather, I will feel liberated and thankful for all that makes my job that much easier and my work that much more interesting.

Jennifer Anderson
Material Series (2006)
Mud, wax, and wood
29" H x 15" W x 19" D (each chair)

Jennifer Anderson
Drove (2006)
Walnut, polyethylene, industrial felt
21" H x 15" SH x 20" W x 20" D (each chair)

Susan Working
Soapbox (2005)
Cherry wood, paint, copper, soap, paper, mirror
9" H x 23.5" W x 5.5" D

The words printed on the soap were taken from the front page of the *New York Times* one day in December 2004. I made this piece in response to my guilt and depression over the war in Iraq. I hate the war, I hate that I'm paying for it, and I feel powerless to stop it. From where I stand, it appears that familiar forms of anti-war activism are both absent and somehow meaningless or futile.

So I call the piece *Soapbox* and that's the first layer of relationship—a verbal/visual pun that means "to proselytize" and also tries to get across the idea of guilt, cleansing, and purification.

I made it in my studio at Anderson Ranch in Colorado. I ordered the cherry from MacBeath Hardwoods in Salt Lake City, and it was delivered by their driver, Darryll, and unloaded by me, Jason, Tyler, and Alexis. Before that, the cherry was milled and dried in Indianapolis, and it was shipped there from somewhere back East. Before that, it was part of an orchard somewhere.

The paint I used was a mix of milk paint and oils. I think of the cow, her unknown life and the minerals and organic materials that combine to make the colors—the geologic and environmental processes that brought them into being. And the hands that mixed them and made the binders and thinners and the long, long history of knowledge that's held in these tubes and packages.

The copper bowl was spun on a lathe from a used, resin-covered plate I got from our print studio. As I heated and bent the plate a seated Buddha appeared on the inside surface just under the lip. It couldn't have been more perfect or more unexpected—an accidental gift. Unknown to me, the plate was from a William Wiley print, and who knows where he lifted the Buddha image. —*SW*

Why Am I Still Making Stuff
Susan Working, Anderson Ranch, CO

We live in a world overrun by objects, most of which we don't even need. The castaways float off to sea on trash mountains. They pile up in landfills. They heat up the atmosphere.

Who really wants all this stuff?

The multiplication of objects is driven by displaced desire. The cogs of our lives are moved by the wheel of endless production. Capitalism converts longing into consumption, with the promise of satisfaction always deferred. We fantasize movement from an imagined past to an imagined present as progress. Official histories fabricate chronologies that bring retrospective order to the dreamy chaotic jumble of everyday experience.

What if, instead of such a vision, we imagine history as multiple, contradictory and fluid, and ourselves as permeable and available to this multiplicity? What would that suggest about the practice and purpose of adding to the clutter of objects in the here and now? What if we think of object-making as a practice in anarchic thinking? Something that scrambles our confidence in the idea of progress, that teaches us to simultaneously hold on to hope

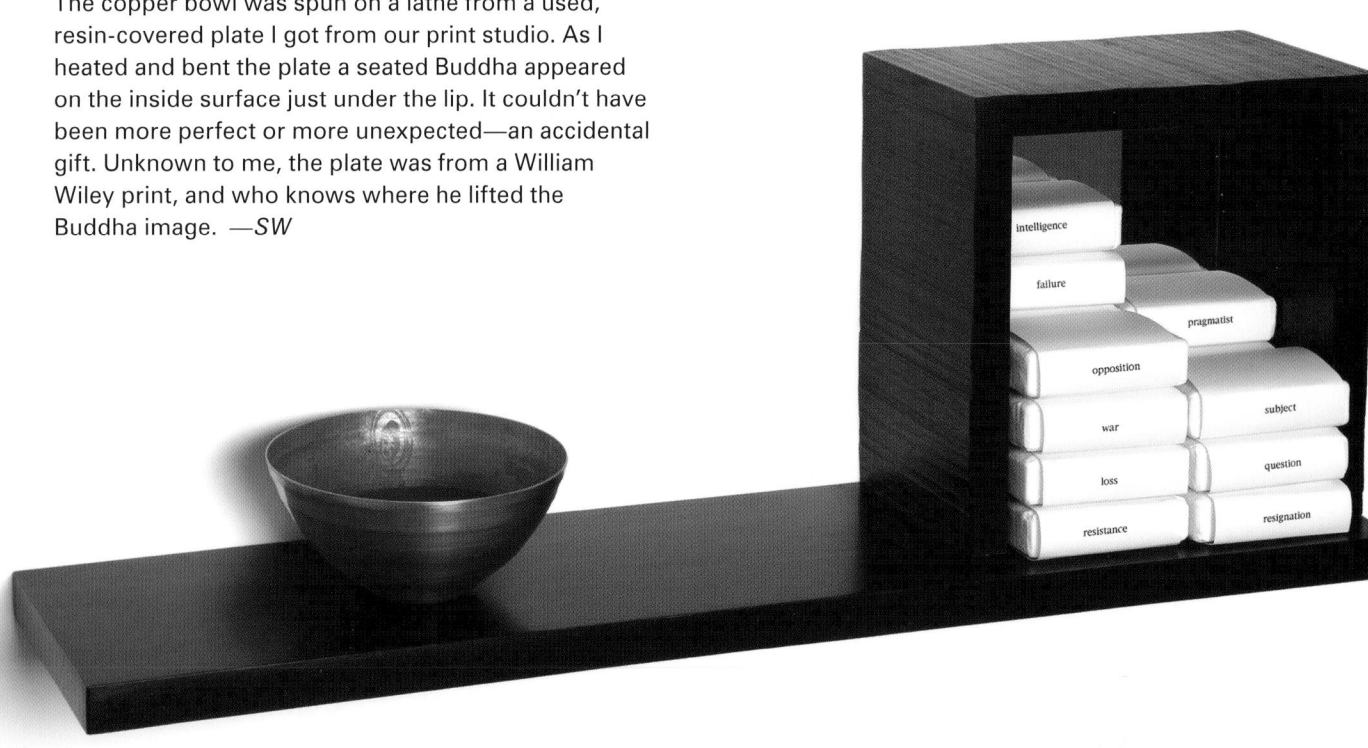

and the possibility of its erasure? What if we think of ourselves as mediums, calling up ghosts?

At the moment, I've embraced an anarchic method of working: no worked-out drawings, no ordered master plan. Just an improvisational process that's a collaboration between intention, physical effort, skills, technology, materials, and time and place. Of course, any making process, however well-planned, involves improvisation. Making is always a collaborative act, even when we do it alone. After the fact, we apply a narrative of conquest, of expertise. But in practice, the act of making is a lesson in humility: of adjustment and compromise. The process debunks the illusion of individual control and affirms a collaborative truth at the heart of living: the fact of its inevitable condition of relationality, and the density of relationships it activates.

The medium of furniture is fundamentally ghostly. Pieces of furniture are our collective phantom limbs. This may be one reason that in this culture, we find the one-off alluring, expressive, and personal. This ghostliness interests me. I like to concern myself with the role of the medium—the wood-medium as clairvoyant—in summoning ghosts past and present. I like to concern myself with furniture-hauntologies. I'm drawn to the work that elicits buried voices.

Art involves not only producing relationships with the world—including, of course, social relationships—but also in revealing or manifesting relationships that already exist, that sometimes have a long history of existence, relationships that pertain not only to objects but to processes, substances, life forms, and histories swept away by time.

Creation is Ideal But Evolution is Real
Daniel Michalik, Long Island City, NY

The work I have been making for the past few years resides in a strange nether-region somewhere between the realms of craft-oriented "studio" furniture and production-oriented design. As a result, it is often difficult for this work to find true acceptance in any specific discipline, each seeing shades of other, incompatible disciplines.

Ultimately, when the unnecessary and useless divisions are stripped away, we see that there is really no such thing as studio furniture, no such thing as design. There is no craft, there is no mass production. Simultaneously, as none of these things exist individually, these things are all that exist when we talk about making things. There are no essential differences between them. They are all shades of the same thing. We must throw away our possessiveness with respect to tradition. Let us share knowledge and change and talk about the objects themselves, rather than being blinded by how they came to be. Studio furniture, design, craft: They are all the same thing, so why do we continue to confuse and divide?

Daniel Michalik
Desk (2006)
Cork
33" H x 72" W x 31" D

Commissioned by the National Museum of the American Indian GGHC-Heyes Center, New York City.

If we are secure enough in our universal ability to create useful objects, we will welcome challenge and subversion. We must understand the strengths, weaknesses, and beauty of that method we call our own. Most of all, we must look beyond ourselves: forward into a bright future in which new methods are invented, new materials are embraced, old materials are rethought, and new experiences are had. We must evolve if we are to survive, and integration and acceptance is the truest path toward true evolution.

Daniel Mchalik
Cub (2006) child's chair
Cork
17" H x 12" W x 13" D

Cork is completely sustainable, regenerating itself every ten years for harvest. It is also recyclable, plentiful, and wonderfully tactile. I have tried to explore the deep potential of the material, making it do things it has never done before, as well as things that only it can do. —DM

An Unwilling Avant-Garde
Don Miller, Philadelphia, PA

Most students I meet ask "Why make more stuff?" The question implies a distance from the subjective experience of making art, tempering it with the identity of what they make as "product." The question suggests an unwillingness to blindly accept the economic assumptions of our medium—the small world of the isolated maker, the gallery, the museum and, most importantly, the identity/authenticity of the handmade.

Youth and optimism empower students to visualize change on a presumably impossible scale. They experience mass culture as participants, at once indulging and distancing themselves. Their interests are intense, nervous, and eclectic. The nature of their cultural experience is constant change, constant spectacle.

Much of the best work involves a rigorous irony—a distancing of the self and perception from making and experience of the object. These are objects made to be looked at, considered parallel to their use, eliciting visceral responses held in tension with social and cultural expectations. They pose insoluble riddles that illuminate new levels of experience and meaning. They intentionally interrogate and interrupt the assumed patterns of daily life, of use, of comfort. They employ the recent past—their parents' childhood, my childhood—as a stylistic reference point for the hyper-normal to be visually disrupted or conflated into trickster hybrids.

In the studio, much of this work involves importing industrial processes and materials, creating new sets of problems—and solutions—that employ the conceptualization rather than the specific manual skills of traditional means. They want to simultaneously master and subvert traditional techniques. Students accept the limitations of "format" of industrial materials as a matter of fact, while throwing themselves repeatedly against the limitations of natural materials.

And yet many of these students are focused on and frighteningly adept at hand processes, and exhibit a profound interest in the character of materials. Their restless commitment to unraveling the past to discover the "next moment" is fueled by an exuberance and fearlessness that I can only dream about. The risk of letting their voices be heard presents an inevitable challenge to the authority of the past they are displacing, one that will evolve the character of our medium.

If the so-called studio furniture movement is to remain relevant to more than an aging constituency, leadership, and audience, it must more willingly grapple with the impulses of the next generation, it must view its interrogation of the past as an opportunity for self-critical reflection, and, most importantly, it must engage in discourse. This conversation must be democratic, rigorous, and include peers across a wider swath of cultural

Don Miller
Teatable (2006)
Bleached white oak
28″ H x 32″ W x 32″ D

opinion and activity. This must take place at all levels of our community—between part-timers and professionals, the self-taught and the over-educated. If not, the attentions of the young will wander. Our values combine in a perhaps uneasy but necessary dialectic, a whole greater than the sum of its parts. It is fundamental for all of us—educators, studio artists, professionals, and hobbyists—to remember that young makers exhibit a desire that we all share: to create work that resonates and is recognized within our constituency and beyond. The risk is real but fundamental. The young will draw us all forward if we let them.

Homespun Ideas

Reinterpreting craft in contemporary culture

by Lydia Matthews

The early 21st century is proving to be a volatile time for the c-word: "craft" seems to be suffering from an identity crisis. Its fans and practitioners are now at a crossroads. Should they assertively maintain what they have believed and practiced internationally for centuries, defending it against those who dismiss their field as quaint or passé? Or would they be better served to radically reinterpret their past and current activities so that craft's future relevance within contemporary culture will be more secure? While those in the craft world argue among themselves about the best way to heighten craft's cultural currency, the powers-that-be in the contemporary global art world—with its penchant for all things critical and "fresh" (which

usually translates as marginal or subcultural)—are eagerly cannibalizing many of craft's techniques, eccentricities, and home-spun ethics, incorporating them into the latest forms of avant-garde practice.

Let me back up and explore how this peculiarly complex morass came into being, and the ways it is manifesting in my own Bay Area back yard. Clearly, there is an undisputable paradigm shift occurring. In 2004, New York's American Craft Museum, arguably the most significant institution to champion the historical legacy of craft practices in the United States, transformed into the "American Museum of Art and Design." About the same time, the Bay Area's California College of Arts and Crafts (CCAC) severed its obvious connection to William Morris's 19th century socialist tradition by renaming itself the "California College of the Arts." Despite its new moniker, the school's kilns, looms, letterpresses, potshop, jewelry/metals, and furniture studios are still fully functional, yet they are now no longer associated with the word "crafts" in the school's public persona.

Some craft enthusiasts regarded the re-branding of these two institutions as an attack on artisan traditions, or at least an overt attempt to make them mute. Others interpreted the organizational makeovers as a sign that craft had finally been

left: Scott Oliver
Moire for Office and Gallery (2005)
Fiberboard, 8'8" H x 21'6" W x 5" D
Photo: Wilfred J. Jones

In the Southern Exposure installation, Oliver replaced the walls separating gallery from office with double-layer perforated fiberboard screens. Moving around the space creates a moire pattern that shifts and shimmers. Since the gallery is an artist-run institution, Oliver's visually striking approach helps break down the barriers that normally separate the viewers from the operating staff.

Editor's Note—*Lydia Matthews is a Brooklyn-based writer, educator, cultural activist, and curator, who co-founded and directed the graduate program in visual criticism as well as the MFA program in fine arts at the California College of the Arts (formerly known as California College of Arts and Crafts). She taught art history, theory, and criticism for 17 years in San Francisco before recently relocating to New York City to become associate dean of educational programs and associate professor at Parsons' The New School for Design. Her writing on contemporary visual culture has appeared in a variety of international publications and her recent curatorial projects include serving as the U.S. curator for the 2005 Art Caucasus International Biennial in Tbilisi, Georgia, where she plans to return in Fall 2007 to co-curate "One Stop," a series of urban interventions created by international artists in shops and storefronts throughout the city.*

This essay was first published in 2006 in the catalog for "Practice Makes Perfect: Bay Area Conceptual Craft," a landmark exhibition organized and presented by the artist-run Southern Exposure gallery in San Francisco.

As gallery director Courtney Fink notes in her curatorial statement, "The artists in the exhibition emulate the

elevated to its deserved status as a legitimate form of contemporary art. For others more versed in the phenomena of global marketing, the revised logos reflected non-profit business strategies. They simply announced themselves as "new and improved" cultural spaces, ones more responsive to the demands of contemporary capitalist culture. With an updated identity that more accurately reflected the expanding sensibility of their programs, they would be better able to solicit and cultivate the audiences they most desire.

But what did these two organizations hope to gain by specifically associating with "Arts" and "Design" instead of "Craft?" There were, of course, many official public relations statements offered to answer this question. But one unspoken truth is that "craft" may conjure things in people's minds that neither place wanted to spotlight as its own. The erasure of "craft" from their titles was a way to distance themselves from the negative stereotypical baggage that it implicitly carries. Many people currently associate "craft" with unique, signature-style vessels, jewelry, wall hangings, or furniture made by hand and sold in chic boutiques, museum

habitual practice that is typically assigned to the realm of craft, but they move beyond it to a very intentional and equal consideration of materials and concept. This way of working merges the utilitarian with the utopian, the subject with the object, and the tangible with the intangible, resulting in work that can be considered Conceptual Craft."

Matthews' lucid essay and the works she discusses, along with the current bubble and seethe in the larger craft world, shine a sideways light on studio furniture, where obsessive craftsmanship combined with artistic vision often results in objects whose function rests upon the embodiment of an idea. As the notion of Conceptual Craft stakes out its place in the larger world of art criticism, much of what we understand to be studio furniture might find a place there too.

It's no coincidence that along with their interest in craft-based work, the curatorial staff at Southern Exposure was extremely obliging in helping Furniture Studio *assemble our coverage. This level of cooperation with the folks next door is rare in the fine arts whirl, and a pleasure to encounter.*

—John Kelsey, editor

shops, craft galleries, and local fairs. These objects embody the legacy of the 1960s and 70s Studio Craft movement, a time when craftspeople tried to reclaim a more authentic way of life by blending Eastern and Western artisan traditions with an alternative back-to-the-land lifestyle, one stubbornly self-sufficient and deliberately poised against the elitism of the art world and its market system. During the last 35 years the Studio Craft movement evolved into a more institutionalized phenomenon, with its own separate galleries, publications, and audiences. But unlike the rest of the art world, which favors critical cultural discourse, the craft world's cultural forums have been largely celebratory. As a result, many of the objects made within this tradition are functional, eye-pleasing, humorous, tasteful, even inventive—but they can err on the side of the pretty, or fun, rather than the astute. Such work is often critically dismissed because it fails to deliver a significant conceptual punch or the kind of rigorous social critique demanded by many contemporary culture aficionados.

To make matters worse, the c-word may evoke images of funky DIY hobbyist activities, spin-offs from the 1970s Studio Craft movement. Envision spider plant hangers made of brown hemp macramé, quilted patchwork plaid country kitchen napkin holders, or tissue dispensers that children bring back from their summer camp's craft class,

Christian Maychack
Untitled (2005)
Mixed media, variable dimensions
Photo: Wilfred J. Jones

The bricks come to life in Christian Maychack's installations, writhing and flowing and finally freezing into perfect crystals of wallboard. The artist makes meticulous replicas of the original materials, leaving the viewer to guess what is real and what is not—or to suspend belief and enter into the spirit of the work.

ones adorned with glued macaroni noodles. These informal objects become instantly retro within the vernacular environment of the home, and are sentimental signifiers of folksy nostalgia.

Of course there are many problems with this cursory dismissal of the Studio Craft tradition. For one, does the lack of critical rigor associated with craft actually reside in the mind of its maker or is it located within the art viewer's capacity to perceive the conceptual richness of a crafted object? Might content be located in the artist's aesthetic attitude rather than in the object's forms or materials alone? Is an object's cultural and economic worth determined entirely by its display context or rhetorical framing? Any way you look at it, the significant subtext here is that "serious cultural practice" has become virtually synonymous with conceptually-oriented art, which usually translates as work made by academically trained artists, championed by blue-chip galleries, circulated internationally by theoretically oriented curators, and reviewed by critics who write for influential journals. It often looks visually spare, conveying all of the elegance and sophistication of its sanctioned Modernist predecessor, Minimalism. This kind of work favors an educated audience, one willing to enter the art world regularly and speak its specialized mother tongue.

Whereas conceptual gallery art caters to what used to be called a highbrow elite, the kinds of problematic craft objects I described above manifest a middlebrow or lowbrow legacy. "Design," on the other hand, distinguishes itself from the practices of "fine art" and "craft" by unabashedly foregrounding its relationship to mass production within the global marketplace. Designers cater to a specific business client who wants to sell things to people for use in their daily lives—an act that used to be executed by a craftsperson in years past. Design manifests what cultural critic John Seabrook described as a "nobrow"[1] phenomenon, fusing and confusing these categorical distinctions by borrowing aspects from each. For example, designers may deliberately highlight their individual names (e.g., "Alessi" or "Graves")— essentially offering Modernist or Postmodernist credentials familiar in the art world—but these signatures have now been transformed into brand logos, reproduced for huge audiences, perhaps even made in factories abroad. Moreover, design is less dependent on display to garner its meaning, seeming at home within a wide range of commercial environments. A chirping teapot or elegant halogen lamp might be found in a gallery like Limn or the MOMA store, and then again in mail-order catalogues for Design Within Reach, or big-box chain stores including Ikea or Target.

While the categories of "art" and "design" are currently stereotyped and packaged as urban, hip, sexy, potentially transgressive, technologically savvy, intellectually astute, and politically progressive, "craft" is cast as fundamentally down-to-earth, time-honored, conventional,

non-threatening, and conservative by comparison. Craft is like welcomed comfort food when compared to art and design's upscale gourmet meal, the former spooned into a brown-glazed earthenware bowl and the latter presented vertically on an Italian porcelain plate—served up with all of the economic class connotations

Stephanie Syjuco
By Any Means Available (after Charlotte Perriand) (2005) *(left)*
Paper, cardboard, tape, collage, mixed media, 84" x 73" x 14"
La Maison Tunisie (after Perriand) (2004) *(right)*
Paper, cardboard, tape, collage, mixed media, 100" x 48" x 13"
Photo: Wilfred J. Jones

By mimicking the elegant and once aesthetically revolutionary Modernist designs of Charlotte Perriand, Syjuco fabricates her display cases out of reconfigured remnants of Ikea furniture and tattered scrap materials. Her work offers a commentary on the battered legacy of the International Style and the "make-do" impulse so often witnessed within the built environment of Third World cities.

and Eurocentric assumptions suggested by that analogy. In a fast-paced, upwardly mobile, star-oriented visual culture like ours, it isn't hard to understand why people in the craft world might be feeling devalued by the mainstream right now.

Then again, they may simply be ahead of the curve. Within the context of globalized factory production and an excessively consumerist culture, it becomes possible again to appreciate the simplicity and meticulousness of craft precisely because it privileges an unhurried and imaginative process. Perhaps patiently making one thing by hand is, in fact, a radical act in our dominantly high-speed, hyperactive, digital age of multi-tasking. Moreover, craft's aesthetic marginality is proving to be at the heart of its potential appeal to wider audiences. Ironically, at the exact moment when some craft-oriented institutions are re-branding in order to distance themselves from the problematic sides of their historical legacy, key elements within the contemporary art world are putting forth the opposite proposal. Craft may be on the brink of becoming the international art world's newest sub-cultural "Other."

Poised for reinterpretation

Several recent events point to the fact that craft is poised for reinterpretation. Artists and curators throughout the world are already mining it in sophisticated ways. Take, for example, the prestigious Turner Prize. Reserved for the most significant British contemporary artist, it was awarded in 2004 to a rural "self-trained potter," whose clay vessels conveyed edgy sexual narratives. One year later, the Turner Prize went to Jeremy Deller, a young artist known for championing the aesthetics of what he calls "contemporary folk art:" visually odd stuff or striking performance events crafted by ordinary people, often (but not always) those who live in rural provinces. What caught Deller's eye were the things people made to facilitate their local festivals, holidays, or daily lives. Deller's practice includes researching and curating these "authentic" folk expressions, taking them into his archive as Duchampian readymades and re-contextualizing them within the hallowed halls of the Tate Modern and other venues. When Ralph Rugoff, then curator of San Francisco's Wattis Institute of Contemporary Art, invited Deller to become the Capp Street Artist in Residence in 2004, the artist spent much of his time focused on the socio-aesthetic practices of Oakland's Black Panther Party. This aspect of "folk" visual culture was one part of what Deller regarded

as a fascinating living history within the exotic American West, worthy of the art world's attention and a critical intervention within its traditional framework.

There is another side to this current fascination with craft made by ordinary—albeit creative—folk. In innumerable recent gallery exhibitions, academically trained artists like Tim Hawkinson, Tara Donovan, or Dinh Q. Lê are featured for their labor-intensive processes. These artists' fastidious and repetitive techniques pay homage to the intensity of concentration and dexterous skills required of various craft traditions. Like an accomplished metalsmith, Hawkinson meticulously assembles fingernail cuttings to form a perfectly surreal skeleton of a bird. Donovan unpacks thousands of white plastic drinking cups and carefully suspends each from the ceiling at slightly varied length, creating a gently rolling topography that envelops its audience. Dinh Q. Lê, who is based in Ho Chi Minh City, cuts his large-format stills from Hollywood films about the Vietnam/America War into thin strips, weaving them together with other local images from that historical period, in the technique he learned from the women basketmakers in his family. Though these artists use unconventional materials to make their monumental, other-worldly creations, they still mimic the obsessive or meditative practice that most craftspeople have always valued and perpetuated.

This is not a craft-for-craft's sake aesthetic practice, or a purely intuitive act. It involves an active commitment to slowing down, focusing on the rhythm of physical movements, carefully observing what is materially present within the process, and patiently executing a craft technique in the service of an overall concept. It is what manifests in David Ireland's classic *Dumballs*, a work in which the artist tossed a handful of thick cement back and forth in the air until it formed a perfect sphere that fit into his palms, creating seemingly identical balls over and over again. Ireland's is a literal act of using one's hands to meditate on a specific subject matter and evoke it formally. To accomplish this, an artist might use tools ranging from the ancient to the digital. This fusing of technical method,

Bernie Lubell
Conservation of Intimacy (2005),
above, foreground, installation view; *right*, detail
Pine, birch, maple latex, music wire, springs,
copper, and nylon line
Photo: Tyson Washburn

Bernie Lubell's amazing Rube Goldberg contraption
spans the installation at Southern Exposure. When you
(or two of you) sit on the wooden bench above, your
weight trips a pneumatic sensor and drives automatic
pencils pressing on a stream of paper that flows down
the wall at right. When you jiggle and squirm, the
pencils respond. Although highly sophisticated and
complex in its actions, Lubell does not fuss over the
fit and finish of his machines, preferring rough edges
and ends, and with them, a non-preciousness that
invites interaction.

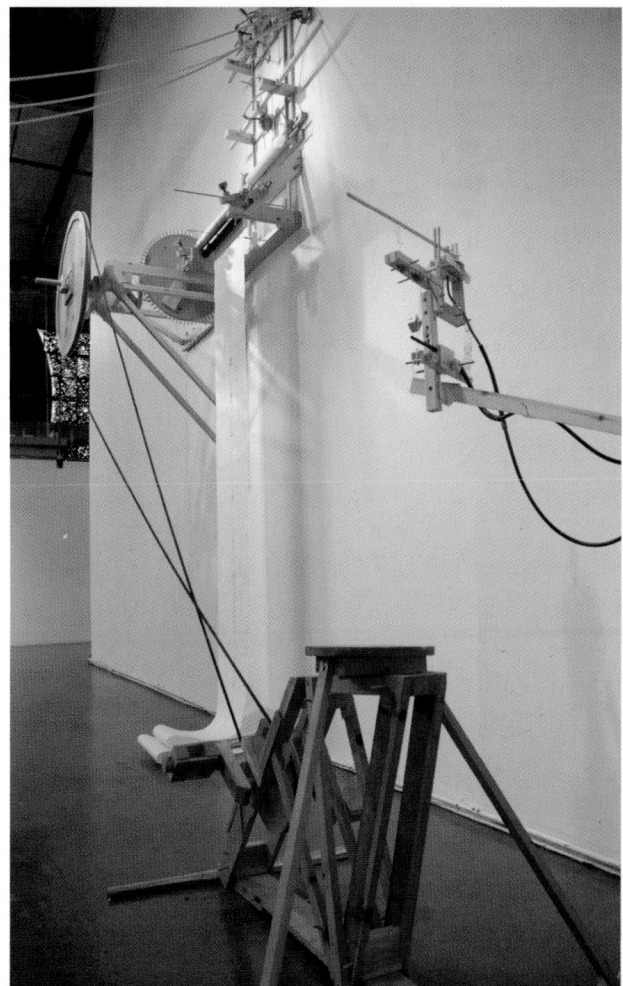

Tony Tredway
dumb (2003)
Variable dimensions; ultralight medium-density fiberboard,
plastic laminate, plastic fast-caps

Tredway uses the language of Victorian gingerbread architecture, so
prevalent in San Francisco, to create mysterious pathways that meander
across the walls and encounter strange boxes, platforms, and openings.
Tredway mills the mouldings to suit the installation, to subvert the eye
of the viewer and take him or her on the artist's secret mission.

a keen sense of design and poignant subject matter morphs into a third space we might call "Conceptual Craft."

Conceptual Craft

The artists featured in "Practice Makes Perfect: Bay Area Conceptual Craft" are similar in sensibility to Hawkinson, Donovan, and Lê (who only represent the tip of the iceberg of this globally omnipresent aesthetic). Southern Exposure's curators demonstrate that Conceptual Craft, while not unique to this region, has a strong history in the Bay Area and is being practiced widely today. Some of the artists in this exhibition began their careers with an aesthetic background in traditional craft or design. For example, Anna Von Mertens' hand-dyed and stitched Minimalist sculptures, superimposed with images of atomic clouds created by an architectural AutoCAD program, initially grew out of a quilt-making practice. Others in the exhibition honed their craft and design skills within their professional trades as well as their studios: Bernie Lubell's eccentric, psychologically loaded, interactive wood sculptures serve as a complement to his longstanding practical work as an accomplished carpenter. In his studio work, he is able to harness his woodworking and construction skills to a more imaginative end. Similarly, Amy Franceschini has worked since the mid-1990s as a graphic/web designer, now combining project-based digital design with more hands-on sculpture. Her client-based practice and experience within the company she founded, www.futurefarmers.com, may have influenced her interest in collaborative, interactive work in the public sphere. Franceschini and Michael Swaine's current project is an example of this kind of social practice: it embraces a community-oriented Arts and Crafts ethic by both engaging local shoemakers and playfully improvising on their designs.

After a longstanding infatuation with what local art critic Glen Helfand dubbed San Francisco's "Mission School" (i.e., a fusion of graffiti art, hip-hop/hobo aesthetics, with a nod to the legacy of la Raza muralismo and a skateboarder's sense of urban space and communal ethics), the curators at Southern Exposure may be looking to establish the prevalence of other Bay Area art practices (after all, collectors are always in search of a new twist.) While Conceptual Craft is no born loser, it is wise to re-introduce it to the cultural scene as a kind of refined cousin of the Mission School.

Conceptual Craft stems from a separate historical trajectory, yet both are linked by a keen awareness of contemporary art and design practices.

While the artists in "Practice Makes Perfect" vary widely in generation, disciplinary background, and intellectual interests, they all share a particular kind of art education: they are versed in the history of Modernist fine art, Postmodernist critical theory, and the diverse hybrid practices that make up the contemporary art world. We see these art historical sources quoted directly in works by Stephanie Syjuco, who synthesizes high signature-style Modernist forms by masters like Frank Lloyd Wright and Charlotte Perriand with Ikea furniture remnants to comment on a third-world, black market economy. They also appear in Tony Tredway's use of custom-milled Victorian molding and Formica, compositions formally inspired by Minimalist color field painting, as well as Christian Maychack's obsessive nod to 1920s Surrealism in his exquisite architectural growths, seamlessly molded as if manifesting their own peculiar logic. Scott Oliver's perforated gallery wall combines a Gordon Matta-Clark architectural cutting gesture and a decorative Art Nouveau-inspired pattern. Oliver's intervention makes the gallery's administrative offices more visibly a part of the exhibition space, allowing the two sides of the wall to become permeable in order to acknowledge the labor involved in cultural activity—a piece that pays homage to previous institutional critiques by Richard Serra and Chris Burden, among others.

Through contact with influential Bay Area art school mentors like Jim Melchert, David Ireland, Mark Thompson and Ann Chamberlain—critically minded and fundamentally interdisciplinary teachers as well as internationally recognized artists—at least three generations of artists have been groomed to make research-oriented, architecturally sensitive, conceptually driven work. Like these mentors, their students focus attention on keenly observing/representing the present moment. Chamberlain's meticulous paper-piercing ultimately creates a field of light so the viewer may track the rotations of the sun within the gallery's architecture, a phenomenon that

Mark Thompson
A House Divided (1989) (top)
Performance and installation
The Sixth Sense (Closing a Sale) (2005) (above)
Single-channel video
Photo: Wilfred J. Jones

For thirty years, Thompson has collaborated with honeybees in his artistic process. In his seminal work, *A House Divided*, he built a structure that enabled him to place his head into the world of the bees while they built their hive. In *The Sixth Sense (Closing a Sale)*, the bees gradually accumulate on the artist's gesturing, pheromone-coated hands. Finally they obscure his gestures entirely and transform the communication from a human sign language to one of their own.

is at once immaterial and in flux. Much about this approach to making—like the way Melchert deliberately invites and highlights accidents in an otherwise regulated process, or Thompson's physical interaction with bees and his poignant bodily gestures that communicate without using words—are rooted in aesthetic experiments of the 1950s through the present. During the last half-century, these and other prominent Bay Area artists have openly explored Buddhist philosophies and meditative practices, alongside conceptual art proposals coming from New York and Los Angeles, as well as outside the United States.

Participatory knowledge

What has been privileged in this kind of work and teaching is what might be called "participatory knowledge:" the accumulated memory produced through direct practice within one's body rather than through deductive rational methods alone.[2] Often inspired by a hunch or an intuition, this kind of knowledge produces unexpected discoveries. It invites playful improvisation precisely because it is based on a excessively disciplined technique that has been confidently internalized. It delights in the act of repeatedly making and remaking, inventing fresh images and objects. This form of conceptualism does not pit the mind against the

body, but rather manifests the intricate relationship between the two.

Participatory knowledge is a phenomenon explored not only by Bay Area artists, but also by philosophers and psychologists at the University of California, Berkeley. In Professors George Lakoff and Mark Johnson's fascinating book, *Philosophy in the Flesh: The Embodied Mind and Its Challenge to Western Thought*, they propose that the basic anchors of our conceptual system are models of direct human agency—pushing, pulling, hitting, throwing, lifting, giving, taking, and so on—all fundamentally embodied experiences.[3] Our literal and metaphorical conceptualization of the world is accessed through replaying or "playing" physical movement. This is a phenomenon well understood by anyone engaged in a reflective craft practice, as Christopher Rose (chair designer and professor at the University of Brighton) described in a publication produced jointly by Haystack Mountain School of Crafts and the Massachusetts Institute of Technology Media Lab.[4]

Recognizing the importance of these and other interdisciplinary ideas coming out of the Bay Area and elsewhere at the millennium, the Center for Craft, Creativity and Design in Hendersonville, North Carolina, organized a series of annual "Craft

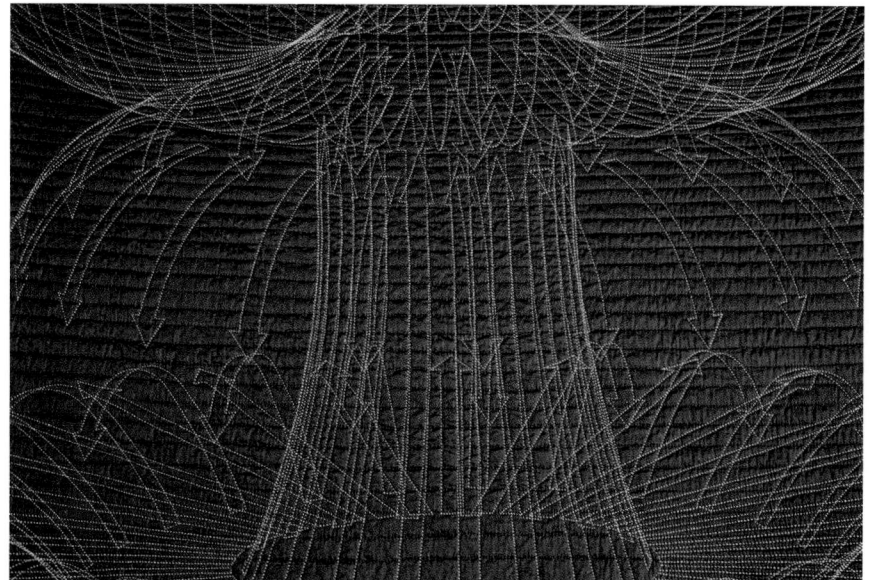

Anna Von Mertens
Black and White (2004), overall *(left)* and detail *(above)*
Hand-stitched cotton, 60" x 80" x 17" (each piece)
Photos: Wilfred J. Jones

The energy pattern of a nuclear explosion adorns these bed-sized sculptures, meticulously hand-stitched with white thread on the black quilt and black thread on the white. But while the black quilt looks into the teeth of destruction, the white one looks down on the same information— a startling transformation that resembles a mandala of peace.

Think Tanks." I participated in two recent national retreats, alongside a dozen other artists, scholars, curators, art administrators, educators, and critics. For three days each year, we debated the status of craft in contemporary visual culture. Here are my conclusions:

First, thinking in terms of "art versus craft versus design"—with segregated cultural forums—is dull and outmoded. Better to envision how these ways of making overlap, synthesize, or resist one another's aesthetic assumptions. And yet while these disciplinary boundaries are increasingly eroding, each practice is rooted in unique cultural histories that should be remembered distinctly. Each field merits equal critical attention. Fine arts educators must therefore reevaluate the significance of both craft and design histories so that Conceptual Craft is not cast as yet another subcultural flavor of the month. On the other hand, craft practitioners and critics would do well to become more theoretically versed and conscious of how their traditions function within contemporary culture. How does their work operate in relation to global economic systems, scientific theory, philosophy, popular culture, new/mass media, cultural tourism networks, etc.?

Recently we have all seen hordes of twenty-something-year-old screenagers eagerly clicking knitting needles with more passion for the craft than their great-grandmothers before them. Why is this re-appropriation of craft such an omnipresent trend in the early 21st century, not only on the streets but also within cultural forums? Perhaps it is because we humans harbor a deep need to experience ourselves as inventive makers of our world rather than just capitalist consumers, driving to the mall or clicking on the "purchase now" icon on the computer. It is comforting— even mesmerizing—to physically enact a repetitive gesture, one that is simultaneously age-old, current, and fruitful. As "Practice Makes Perfect" demonstrates, the primal and playful act of crafting things with precision allows us to dynamically explore significant ideas in our daily lives.

Notes

1. John Seabrook, *Nobrow: The Culture of Marketing, The Marketing of Culture* (New York: Vintage Books, 2001)

2. "Participatory knowledge" is a phrase coined by Arnold Pacey in his book *Meaning in Technology*, paraphrased by Tom Joyce in *Digital Dialogues 2002: Technology and the Hand*, (Deer Isle, Maine: Haystack Mountain School of Crafts and the Massachusetts Institute of Technology Media Lab, 2004, p. 11)

3. George Lakoff and Mark Johnson, *Philosophy in the Flesh: The Embodied Mind and Its Challenge to Western Thought* (NY: Basic Books, 1999, pp. 23-24)

4. *Digital Dialogues 2002: Technology and the Hand*, (Deer Isle, Maine: Haystack Mountain School of Crafts and the Massachusetts Institute of Technology Media Lab, 2004)

News Flash

The future is a giant meteorite... and the craft world has already been hit

by Bruce Metcalf

I found the ACC's national craft conference, called "Shaping the Future of Craft," to be a mixed bag, not so much a sustained meditation on the future but more a series of reports on the present. The most prevalent theme was hybridization. A steady drumbeat of hybrid objects played in multiple PowerPoint presentations. Most were sculpture installations that used one craft material or another. An equally steady drumbeat of subtexts emerged: Young artists choose craft mediums along with the other things they find, buy, or make. The hottest art schools encourage students to freely mix mediums. The rigorous instruction of craft disciplines is obsolete, and the crafts as we know

them are dead. The future of craft, according to these prognosticators, looks a lot like Art-with-a-capital-A, the Art you see in art magazines and in mongo Art exhibitions.

Some teachers in the audience were disturbed by this scenario. Having devoted their lives to transmitting craft skills to younger generations, it was a tad distressing to hear that their work will soon be irrelevant, and that craft studios will be reduced to service components in schools of one-size-fits-all post-conceptual art.

However, a modest set of counter-proposals were presented at a much lower volume. Some came from craft teachers (Rosanne Somerson, professor of furniture design at Rhode Island School of Design, and Lisa Gralnick, professor of metals and jewelry in the art department at the University of Wisconsin-Madison being the most notable), some from young working ceramists, and one from a store owner in the audience. I was far more interested in what these people had to say. While the picture they presented was fragmented, the possibilities they offered were richer and more complex that the main storyline about hybridization. Each of them, in a different way, questioned the received truths of the (largely academic) view that craft must inevitably dissolve into Art practice. Somerson talked at length about her students' interest in small manufacturing ventures; Gralnick insisted that craft is a repository for the sensual experience. And Amy Shaw, the shop owner, observed that there is a tremendous interest in craft as a consumer item among her clientele in Brooklyn. Taken along with some trends I have observed out in the real world, a different picture of the future of craft emerges.

Embracing design and industry

The current generation of students have no use for categories. The pigeonholes of craft, design, and art are nearly meaningless to them. The most interesting project is to blur boundaries, to make objects that operate in gray areas. While many are interested in blurring the craft/art boundary, I'm not. Craftspeople have wanted to cross that particular boundary for four decades now. Been there, done that. I am far more intrigued by those who want to mess with the border between craft and design. Of the two boundaries, this one has been explored much less.

Those who know the story of Modernism in the United States know that there was once a major push to have craftspeople design for industry. The move was based on the Bauhaus notion that a designer who has an intimate working knowledge is better qualified to design objects made in that material. The ideal role models for the craftsman-designer were Charles and Ray Eames. But sometime in the 70s, the ideal faded. Not only did students lose interest in working for industry, but industry lost interest in hiring craftspeople. They had young industrial designers with college degrees to choose from, after all. Until about 10 years ago, the two camps had little further contact in this country.

Meanwhile, European designers found they could collaborate with small shops, producing limited editions of inventive designs (see Craft and the Designer, page 58). Or, large companies like Alessi provided the money and connections to get designers to work with craft shops. Some of the objects that emerged from these cooperative ventures received a lot of good press. Examples: all that Memphis furniture, or Marc Newson's 1986 *Lockheed Lounge*.

(left) Cortiça cork chaise lounge, 2006, by Daniel Michalik

Michalik was one of Rosanne Somerson's students at Rhode Island School of Design. He's interested in the possibilities of manufacturing his furniture, and has located a small shop in Portugal to produce some of his designs for cork furniture, presumably including *Cortiça*. His attitude is nothing like that of a typical industrial designer: Michalik believes that hands-on experience with a material is essential to good design. And yet, he has no qualms about taking his hands away from the production phase, and exploiting whatever technical means are suited to the job. He relates his approach to the Shakers, especially to their chair-making venture in Mount Lebanon, NY. In effect, he is a proponent of the Bauhaus ideal of craft training for industrial design— the same ideal that Aileen O. Webb tried so hard to instill into American crafts during the 1940s and 50s.

Editor's Note—*Bruce Metcalf, a jeweler and writer who lives near Philadelphia, attended the American Craft Council conference, "The Future of Craft," held in Houston during September 2006. Metcalf is currently working on a history of 20th century American studio craft, with the art critic Janet Koplos, and because of this background Furniture Studio invited him to react to what he saw and heard at the ACC event.*

Metcalf wishes to thank furniture maker Daniel Michalik, gallery owner Amy Shaw, and Carmine Branagan, executive director of the American Craft Council, for their many insights into the present and future of craft.

Elliott Hundley, *Installation for Hammer Projects*, 2006, The Armand Hammer Museum of Art and Culture Center, Los Angeles. Photo by Joshua White, courtesy of the Hammer Museum.

Hundley's installation for the Hammer Projects series exemplifies the kind of amorphous sculpture/craft practice that was widely touted at the Houston ACC conference. According to the Hammer Projects website, "Elliott Hundley creates collages from thousands of cut-up magazines, personal photographs, drawings, and a variety of commonplace objects including feathers, strings, and twist ties. With titles that often refer to classical drama and mythology, each work represents a fantastical world full of cryptic imagery and meaning." Here, craft practice is reduced to bit player in a larger scheme of semiotic play. In this scheme, craft is handy sometimes, but ultimately disposable.

The under-30 crowd pays attention. The American segregation of design and craft looks increasingly foolish to them. Confident of their abilities, they believe the two disciplines are closely related, and any reasonably skilled individual can cross from one to the other. Furthermore, they think that they can find a way to put their own designs into production even if the big manufacturers ignore them. Who needs Herman Miller? Poke around on the web, and maybe you can find a company interested in working with you.

Some young craftspeople regard themselves as designers. Their training in their medium gives them skills they need to generate good designs, along with sensitivity to cultural issues. The isolation of craft from design looks foolish: they can design, they can think, so why not? Furthermore, they are fearless about technology. Anything that does the job well is good, whether it is digital or hand-based. The precious politics of handwork, the heavy breathing about quality and integrity that once motivated thousands to take up woodworking, has become *passé*. If anything, craft is understood in Bauhaus terms, as a sound training-ground for designing in a particular material. It's a practical orientation, not an idealist one.

Any interest in design leads directly to production for the marketplace. For decades, most craft students mirrored their teacher's attitudes: engaging the market as an "artist" was okay because it was principled, idealistic. But some teachers implied by instruction and by example that design for production was not okay. The purity of art would be stained by commerce. While this was not universally true of woodworking and furniture programs, the attitude was pervasive elsewhere. Not only was the argument flawed—galleries are merely high-toned stores, after all—but it crippled several generations of talented students. Torn by internal conflict about the desirability of getting into production, they conceived of themselves as artists instead. And when that strategy failed, they dropped out of the crafts altogether. Luckily, many in the current generation reject that argument, and embrace the marketplace enthusiastically. A lot of the most interesting new work is being done with the marketplace in mind. Hundreds of young craftspeople see sales as a path to empowerment in this culture, and they would be gratified to make a nice profit.

Commodification

At the ACC conference, furniture historians Edward Cooke Jr., of Yale University, and Glenn Adamson, of the Victoria and Albert Museum, gave a very polished talk about the history of American craft, and some of the social conditions that formed it. It was one of the high points of the conference, but for me it had a sour note. Cooke and Adamson brought up the issue of commodification, which they defined as the process of an object exceeding its use value by becoming a fetish of sorts. Using studio glass as a convenient whipping-boy, they talked about the marketplace leading glass "down the wrong path" "to a certain frenzy" of careless accumulation. Since the topic of the conference was the future, one might conclude that the marketplace is a corrupting influence on the crafts, and should henceforth be treated something like a snarling wolf in your kitchen.

Well. The concept of commodification leads back to Marxism, and the presumption that the marketplace is inherently evil. (It leads further to socialist revolution, and condemnation of the middle class for standing in revolution's way.)

Perhaps Cooke and Adamson believe that commodification is dangerous only at high price points, and small-money capitalism is OK. But an object sold for $10 is no less implicated in the marketplace than another sold for $100,000. Which is the greater distortion: that a craftsman designs a chair to be sold for $50, as Walker Weed once did, or that some real estate developer buys a glitzy piece of glass for $250,000? The marketplace is more than happy to sell expensive quasi-sculptures to self-satisfied nouveaux riches. It's a feedback loop, reinforcing certain kinds of taste, that's all. Nobody is compelled to participate.

I suspect that talk about commodification is actually a way to avoid the issue of bad taste among collectors. Art has acquired importance beyond its use-value for millenniums, and slick marketing has been with us for centuries. No big deal. What's disturbing to elitists like me is that dreadful work sells so well. But we can't attack taste, so we shift our disgust into complaining about commodification.

Urban hipster taste

A radical shift in taste is taking place. I don't know how much this shift is acknowledged at art schools and exhibitions. Some college teachers and craft professionals don't get it, and they tend to suppress every manifestation of this taste whenever it appears. Thinking it's bad, they tend to squash it unthinkingly. However, taste is a companion to both aesthetic sensibility and philosophical outlook, and if a whole bunch of young people buy into a new kind of taste, oldsters had better pay attention.

For lack of a better label, I'll call it urban hipster taste. It has been around for more than two decades, and has been gathering energy of late. For a primer in urban hipster taste, check out a catalog from Archie McPhee. It's all there, in fascinating detail. Urban hipster taste is a confluence of semiotics, shopping, and kitsch. It is often wrapped in irony and humor. It's also quite serious, and has profound implications for the future of craft.

Everybody younger than 30 has grown up in an ocean of signs. They swim in it like fish, hardly noticing it. Think high-speed channel surfing: one context follows another in rapid succession, each one demanding interpretation. Old fogeys like me linger on every channel, puzzled. Why is there a channel devoted to bass fishing? What are all these jump-cut images? Is Christian broadcasting serious, funny, or sad? It all seems to border on incoherence.

Younger people know how to read these signs rapidly, without breaking a sweat. They are all trained semioticians. (Semiotics regards objects and behaviors as all having the properties of language. For instance, we all know the language of cars. Everybody knows what a Rolls Royce means in comparison to a rusty 1989 Dodge.) All under-30s know that no object or image is inert, but is full of meaning and packed with hidden agendas. My generation wondered if the world was meaningless. This generation, in contrast, has to deal with a glut of meaning. They regard meaning as an endless variety of assembly kits. You can do whatever you want with meaning: buy into it, reject it, modify it at will. It's the third option—to treat meaning as a plastic material to be customized at will—that is most commonly accepted.

The semiotic viewpoint tends to flatten meaning, to treat all meanings as roughly equivalent. And interchangeable. People like me, who think of meaning as something one must struggle to find, and who base their lives on one or two central beliefs, find this *laissez-faire* attitude towards meaning almost shocking. Don't laugh. If you're reading this article, you are probably a true believer in the inherent meaning of craft. Or that wood should be treated with reverence. Or that art has transcendent value. To a believer, the proposition that meaning can be taken up and abandoned freely is pretty damn weird.

Shopping

The activity that most closely matches the sense that meaning is exchangeable is shopping. To many young people, shopping and constructing a personal identity are almost the same thing. One shops for clothes that signify a certain attitude, or one mixes different clothes to invent new hybrid identities. Similarly, one shops for furnishings, music, cosmetics or whatever with the same attitude. At the same time, it's clear that these objects are replaceable—they can be exchanged for another set of consumer goods that signify a whole new identity. And given the deluge of consumer goods, there are now so many choices that the permutations are infinite. Shopping is fun, entertaining, ironic. To shop is to play with signs. And shopping is the primal metaphor for life in America today.

Hipster shoppers don't believe the hype, though. They understand that consumers are being manipulated, and they know every advertising trick. They tend to regard it all with ironic detachment. Their attitude can easily be mistaken for insincerity, the glib gallows humor of a willing victim. Maybe. But urban hipsters negotiate through media saturation and 24-7 commerce, looking for the energy. Where's the heat? What's interesting in all this chaos?

Kitsch and the new authenticity

Somebody who plays with signs has a flexible attitude towards authenticity. My generation thought authenticity was basic, fixed, and above all honest. The tiller of the soil had an authentic relationship to the earth and its seasons. The tribal shaman had an authentic relationship to the spiritual realm. And the craftsman has an authentic relationship to his materials—and presumably to the larger culture. Authenticity exudes an aura of uncompromising purity, a beacon of honesty for all the world to see. Think of James Krenov planing his wood, carrying on about the integrity of ultra-fine handwork, and insisting his work stands as a repository of virtue.

Mickey Virus (2004), Aya Kakeda. Photo courtesy the artist, www.ayakakeda.com.

An alternative version of craft now: impure, irreverent, inventive, but still object-based. *Mickey Virus* is a book. The text is hand-embroidered on a ribbon, which can be pulled out of the papiér-mâché head. Kakeda thinks of herself as a storyteller, and craft mediums as a useful vehicle. She remarks: "I start out thinking up a story and come up with the best media for the idea. Some of my stories are pretty violent and creepy... Embroidery feels familiar, like something that has always been around your grandma's living room. I like the contrast between the violence and the soothing familiarity."

(From Shu Hung and Joseph Magliaro, editors, *By Hand: The Use of Craft in Contemporary Art*, Princeton Architectural Press, 2007, p. 94)

To the urban hipster, such earnest sermons are laughable. Authenticity is not located in anything fixed. Instead, it is located in consumer goods. Is the real America found in some grumpy refusenik, sharpening his tools amidst the redwoods? Or is it found in the stores and shopping malls? Hipsters vote for the stores every time.

If authenticity can be constructed out of the debris of shopping, the attitude towards the patina of age changes. Since the 1980s, large numbers of people have been fascinated with the signs of antiquity. Wear, weathering, and the residues of ritual were all taken to stand for authentic experience. Think of Stephen Whittlesey's furniture constructed of recycled boats and buildings: the crusty, worn surfaces were interpreted as representing a simpler, more honest time. Whittlesey's furniture is, in effect, the record of an archeological expedition into a lost world. But now, the patina of age no longer makes sense. It's the patina of kitsch that resonates.

Think about it: what is the archeology of shopping? Kitsch. The prodigious energy of bad taste, of American philistine commercialism at its worst. 1950s cars. Chrome-plated appliances. Barbie dolls. What old fogeys recoil from, hipsters embrace. They tend to find the most energy in the decade immediately before they were born, which now means the 60s and 70s. They correctly understand this stuff as an authentic manifestation of consumer culture, and they delight in it. Because outdated consumer goods are not part of their direct experience, it's exotic and amusing. Because it's semiotic in nature, it's available for playful rearrangement. Kitsch is the clay of hipsters. They rub it on everything. There's nothing precious, nothing that can't be mixed or matched. Have a cocktail! Wear a plaid sports coat! Knit a few robots out of cheesy pink yarn!

Hipster DIY

One might think all this irony and irreverence spells the death of craft. Not so. There's a groundswell of urban hipster do-it-yourself (DIY) activity that has attracted the attention of marketers and publishers. Already, at least two magazines

Readymade cover, December 2006
The public face of the new DIY: *Readymade* magazine markets its vision of urban hipster cool. The publisher's goal is to offer an image so kitschy and self-aware—and self-mocking—that their target audience will enthusiastically identify with it. The couch is supposed to be a DIY project, but it would be pretty demanding for an untrained maker. Most of the projects in the magazine are much simpler, ranging from clothing to simple home décor. Still, the retro design vocabulary is clear: The George Nelson clock provides a basic theme and a visual rhyme with the couch cushions. As for those perky models: champagne, white shoes, and puffed sleeves! Who could ask for more?

are devoted to the subject: *Readymade* and *Craft*. From the point of view of a trained craftsman, they appear primitive. But to measure them by the standards that studio crafts have labored so hard to develop is to miss the point. These magazines (presumably) appeal to a population of young men and women who are dissatisfied with pure consumerism. They want to use their hands for something more than whipping credit cards out of a wallet. They want to make things, maybe for the first time in their lives. Sound familiar?

What's fascinating about Hipster DIY is that the stuff in the magazines looks nothing like the stuff in craft publications and fairs. Some of it's silly (a dumbbell made of D-cell batteries, a clock made of an old paint-by-number painting), but some of it is fairly sophisticated. DIY magazines trade in the familiar lifestyle features: record reviews, new products, features on young artists. Their design sensibility is kitschy: the icon of *Readymade* magazine should be the George Nelson *Atomic Wall Clock* from 1949. At the same time, they suggest a resurgence of interest in handcraft that has very close parallels to the 1960s, when all those hairy hippies churned out yards of macramé and tie-dye. The imagery is different, but the impulse is the same.

While most elitists ignore rank amateurs, this resurgence of interest in making is very promising. It has energy. It's sorta cool. The DIY phenomenon can serve as an entry point to a more disciplined study of making. Hipsters (or hipster wanabees) could very well constitute the core of a new generation of students—if only somebody can figure out how to reach out to them, and get them into classrooms.

The possibilities

Even among urban hipster artists, craft has potential. Shopping pales after a while, and one realizes that even in the vast flood of consumer goods, some things can't be bought. The obvious alternative is to invent your own signs—which means you have to make them. (Or have them made, but only established professionals are rich enough to afford that.) While lots of young artists are content with flat images that can be generated on a computer, plenty of others long for the vividness of objects, of real things that can be held in the hand, worn, or tripped over. Still, nobody should expect purity. Chances are good that handmade stuff will be used in combination with found or bought stuff. The possibilities for energetic combinations are endless, even if they are jarring.

The other piece of good news is that a lot of kids are interested in useful things. After several generations of kids who REALLY wanted to be artists, this is a refreshing change. As high-end craft is increasingly devoted to making useless objects, only good for looking at, the utilitarian roots of craft go ignored. If a new generation of students insists on making things they and their friends can actually use, it will be all to the good.

As far as I can tell, neither craft teachers nor practicing craftspeople are prepared for the shift in taste I have described. It looks corny and unsophisticated. In fact, it's engaged and celebratory, a cheerful embrace of the jumble of signs that constitute visual America. The old way of struggling to find one's true voice is simply not part of their equation, and making value judgments is not particularly important. Hipsters—and, in fact, almost all young people today—make their identities out of a patchwork of images and styles. If teachers and craftspeople can't adapt to this new sensibility, they risk becoming irrelevant.

At the ACC conference, there was a lot of muttering going on that craft is dead, and a lot of fear. Maybe a giant meteorite has hit the craft world, and most crafts are fated to become extinct. Maybe craft will become a collection of hobbies, nothing more. Or maybe the field will adapt. So I ask you: is craft a dinosaur, or a mammal?

detail of *46 Drawer Chest*
Jason Howard, Atlanta, GA
p. 45

Show Us Your Drawers

An open and shut case

by Rosanne Somerson

A drawer has the potential to hold mystery as much as content. A closed drawer fills us with anticipation, and as we slide open the box we satisfy our curiosity about what surprises may be revealed. The hint of promise intensifies our interest as drawers may contain the known or the unknown.

Furniture makers dedicated to fine craft often view the well-made drawer as a measure of technical mastery. An exemplar offers the user first a comfortable entry, a finely conceived pull or ornament that complements the hand and responds to the weight and balance of the drawer as it slides open. A smart running system relates box to case, so that a good drawer glides like silk as it unveils its contents. A thoughtful maker provides an automatic stop, so the well-balanced drawer ends its travel without spilling its insides, or worse, falling onto the user or the floor. And on its return, the consummate drawer stops at the exact position to line up with its neighbors or with other parts of the piece. A seemingly simple component has the potential for tremendous complexity, requiring technical mastery and mindful design to synchronously create a perfect experience while enhancing the overall aesthetics of the piece.

Drawers contain. They can also protect, hide, store, preserve, and eventually expose whatever is inside them. Our common fascination with apothecary cabinets, jewelry chests, and other objects made of stacks of drawers is driven by our keen imaginations. What's in all these places?

Bombe Chest of Drawers
Joseph Klosek, Earlysville, VA
Mahogany, poplar, maple, oak
32" x 35" x 22.5"

The bombe form is based on a Dutch design and was used quite frequently in French furniture. This chest of drawers is based on several American pieces from the Boston area that were made during the last half of the 18th century... only a few were made with a serpentine front and drawer sides shaped to fit the case.
—Joseph Klosek

The bombe chest is an ultimate challenge for the cabinetmaker, requiring curve-sided drawers to fit perfectly into a curve-sided chest. *—RS*

Editor's Note—*Rosanne Somerson is interim associate provost for academic affairs, and professor of furniture design, at Rhode Island School of Design in Providence. These notes first appeared in the catalog for The Furniture Society's "Show Us Your Drawers" juried exhibition, at Herron School of Art and Design in Indianapolis, which opened during the Society's 2006 conference. Somerson juried the exhibition, along with furniture designer Vladimir Kagan of New York City, and chief curator Mark Leach of the Museum of Craft + Design in Charlotte, NC. Together the three jurors selected 29 pieces for exhibition, from more than 100 submissions.*

As Somerson explains in her comments, the jurors perforce worked from images only—they were not able to see and touch the actual pieces of furniture in advance of the exhibition. I've attempted to redress that situation by adding brief captions (JK) based on my experience photographing the exhibition, where I was able to interact with the drawers and enjoy their physicality. Additional remarks by Somerson (RS) have also been appended.

—John Kelsey, editor

Breathing Drawers
J. Peter Schlebecker,
Camden, ME
Basswood,
mahogany, cast
silicone rubber
50" x 17" x 20"

I trained as a vocalist in my youth and learned that singing is really all about breathing. This piece expresses deeply ingrained body awareness through a common side effect of a well-fit drawer: air movement caused by the piston-like action of the drawer within its case....
—*J. Peter Schlebecker*

It's startling and delightful to see and hear the silicone panels in the sides and top of the case swell and relax between their muntins. It gives the case an animal quality. The air motion pushes back against the drawer, slowing down the act of opening and closing, which I couldn't stop doing because I wanted to see it breathe some more. —*JK*

What discoveries are to be made as the drawers provide a sort of "peek-a-boo" game of open and close? We make believe—how could an object like this organize the complexity of our lives?

In contemporary manufacture, the complex requirements of drawer construction and integration with the case have been streamlined with plastic molded boxes constructed with integrated slides, or formed wire baskets that allow ventilation. While sometimes developed as cost-cutting measures, these variations from a solid-wood drawer also change the feel of the piece and the user experience. Many low-cost wooden drawers in mass-production utilize plywood or worse, fiberboard, and joining systems such as hardware (screws and connectors) or machined joints. The traditional method of dovetailing solid-wood components showcases not just the maker's skill, but the history of knowledge that takes advantage of the angled sides of the joints to counteract the forces of pulling a drawer and, over time, of potentially loosening a straight-sided joint. As a result, the solid-wood dovetail-joined drawer has become a marker of excellence in contemporary studio work. Not all of the pieces juried into this show utilized traditional technique, but the echo of our cabinetmaking traditions is evident in many of them. Acknowledging long-standing craftsmanship knowledge, or exploring alternatives through careful design, helps to exemplify the significance of studio work in relation to manufactured work.

I found an interesting challenge in jurying an exhibit about drawers through images only. Usually, my evaluation would include the tactile appeal of opening a drawer or of seeing how the contents related to the core design of the piece. None of our jury could use criteria informed by direct experience with the proposed entries.

Instead, we had to establish a set of individual criteria to select objects for this show. In a subject-based show, I am always interested to see novel interpretations of the essential theme. Which work pushed aesthetic or conceptual responses to the notions of drawers? Which pieces incorporated

Bench with Drawer
Howard Werner, Shokan, NY
Cottonwood
22″ x 15″ x 61″ (fully open)

My work is influenced by both classical forms from Greece and Italy as well as primitive carvings from Africa and Oceania. The tools and materials I employ are important to the finished work. My process is evident in the rough chainsawn surfaces and the untouched natural sections of the trees....
—*Howard Werner*

The drawer, or trough, has a massive solidity requiring you to push and drag it out of the bench—a physical involvement not normally required of the furniture user. Made me think about what I might want to put in the drawer. —*JK*

elegant detailing, interesting use of materials, novel engineering, intriguing interpretations of the theme? Whose work made me rethink my assumptions about drawers or the objects that contain them? And which pieces excelled in aesthetic resolution, pleasing proportions, or execution in a manner that matched the voice of the object? Which objects showcased evidence of a clear and well-stated personal investigation? We made our selections based on criteria such as these, as well as on how well we could read the results based on the clarity and professionalism of the provided images.

A controversial selection is an interesting way to explore some of these questions. The jury disagreed at first about the selection of Joseph Klosek's masterfully executed and interpreted *Bombe Chest of Drawers*. As an educator who has

dedicated much of my teaching career to the development of innovative design, I found myself in the surprising position of fiercely defending a beautiful reproduction for its contextual status in the historic lineage of drawer development and the relevance of that in this exhibition.

The *Bombe Chest* presents the quintessential challenge in drawer making. The particular inherent test is how to achieve successful drawers, typically square boxes in square cases, but here all in matched curves. Not only do the drawer fronts need to line up their complex compound curves, but the sides themselves are shaped curves fitted into matching curved cases, with curved dovetails to boot. Matching these curves in one position is demanding enough, but in a drawer, they need to align all along the length of travel—no small feat.

Jurors asked, "Would we put a reproduction of a masterpiece painting in a painting show?" Klosek's beautiful homage here helped me to convince the jury that this piece was worthy as it not only set the tone of historic interpretation at a very high level, but because it showcased the successful achievement of a body of knowledge that should not be lost in contemporary making.

Another piece that plays with the complexities of fitting drawers is J. Peter Schlebecker's *Breathing Drawers*. Here the artist plays with the notion that the ultimate drawer fits so tightly to its case that it prevents space even for air. Therefore as one drawer is shut, the volume of the air inside forces another drawer to puff open. Schlebecker uses this

Untitled
Bob Marsh, Smithville, TN
Wood, cast resin, paint
18″ x 27″ x 9″

This piece investigates the triumvirate of usable furniture forms, representations of the natural world, and the use/viewer of these objects. —*Bob Marsh*

Marsh uses the image of the captured bird to represent emotional experience and to explore the way that personal convenience and utility are sometimes placed above humanistic concerns. —*RS*

fact literally, employing cast silicone rubber sides that expand with the closing and contract with the opening of the drawers, making the cabinet appear to breathe.

Bob Marsh uses the drawer almost as a stage, a backdrop to present the tragic event of a cast resin bird trapped in its construction. Clearly he uses the drawer as a metaphor but incorporates the language of cabinetmaking as a detail of the poetic. The drawer is executed beautifully, and I suppose it would be a droll pun to say that so is the bird. Here the furniture components become vocabulary for a larger vision that is not about utility or service but rather a narrative that the viewer can choose to write or interpret.

Howard Werner's cottonwood *Bench with Drawer* is consistent with many of Werner's other objects. The clear connection to the raw material of the tree is evidence of the artist's deep connection to not just the wood but to its source as a living, growing thing. He expresses his tribute by constructing a piece that utilizes the natural tendencies of dimensional change that result from seasonal drying and shrinkage characteristics. Carved out of a solid volume, the drawer avoids the usual construction of sides, back, and bottom. The drawer requires vertical access, so it is more like a bin than the standard drawer. Yet the sliding reference of opening and closing remains, and the piece asks us to think about exposing the core of the tree. The texture of the bark, the tool marks, and the patterns from the cracking of the wood as it dries all further define the piece, which has been shaped in clear anticipation of how natural characteristics will enhance the form language of the artist.

Heath Matysek-Snyder plays with the intrigue of opening and closing in his *Pulley Box #3*. Two vertical drawers utilize a combined pulley system, forcing each to rely on the other to open or shut. Their codependency causes one internal drawer box to rise as the other falls, or vice-versa. Closed, the boxes are a simple symmetrical presentation, while open they create a dynamic composition of opposites. Matysek-Snyder simultaneously creates an engineered happening while playing with the experience of how what we see changes graphically. There is a suggestion of the psychological here as well, but that potential interpretation is best left to the viewer.

The final group of selected pieces represents an exciting array of approaches and investigations, from the functional to the sculptural, from objects of intimate scale to objects that tower over the viewer, from objects made of one drawer to objects that contain a multitude of drawers. The included works invite us to enjoy various aspects of experience, whether physical, functional, visual, or psychological. As we concluded the selection process, we all felt excited by the range of ideas and approaches that defines the final show, the first of its kind showcasing drawers as a theme of artist exploration. 🪑

(left) Pulley Box #3
Heath Matysek-Snyder, San Diego, CA
Bird's-eye maple, plywood, aluminum,
aircraft cable, steel
48" x 8" x 8" (each piece)

Children are full of amazement. Where adults
may see the laws of physics and various
mechanical principles, children see a vast
world of curiosity. What I am trying to do is
bring the factor of wonder back to life. Using
medieval mechanics I want to put the curiosity
back into the things we cherish.
—Heath Matysek-Snyder

The drawers move smoothly and glide easily
in and out of their cases—before trying it,
I had expected they would rattle and scrape.
There is a neutral position where both are
fully withdrawn, but the cables and pulleys
immediately transmit to both any motion you
apply to either one of them. *—JK*

(left) Small City with Hidden Drawer
Po Shun Leong, Winnetka, CA
Various woods
15" x 15" x 10"

This is about complexities. Like many great
cities in the world, there are many layers of
cultures. What you see is not what you get.
—Po Shun Leong

A sense of complexity is enhanced by the
varied textures of the piece as well as by the
cacophonous forms. Textures using both
machined surfaces and smooth, refined,
and worked surfaces add to the sense of the
cityscape. *—RS*

I found two hidden drawers, only Po Shun
knows how many more there are. What's most
intriguing about his city boxes is, the closer
you look, the more there is to see—just like
a living organism. *—JK*

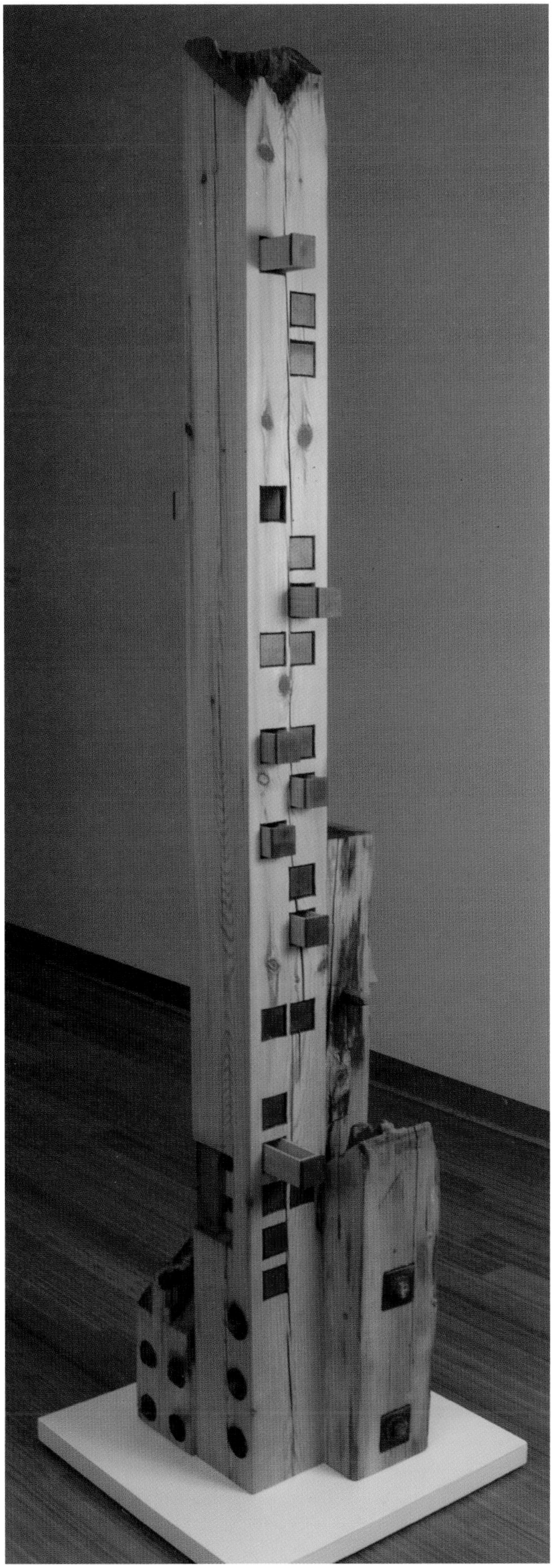

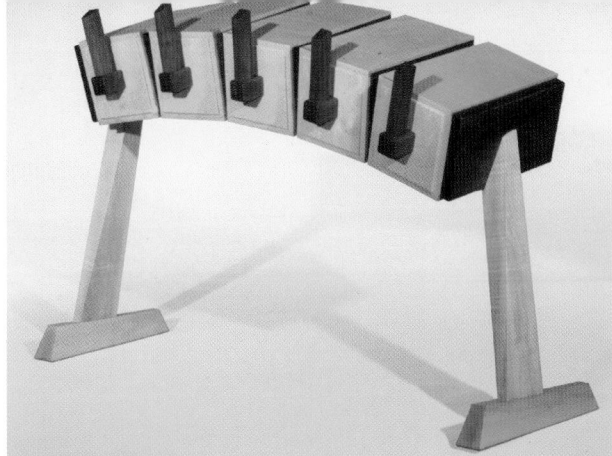

(above, detail at right)
Squeeze Box
J. Speetjens,
Greensboro, NC
Accordion reeds,
rock maple, black
walnut, poplar
34.5" x 56" x 22"

The relation of
cabinetmaking to
instrument making
is not often integrated in contemporary work, although
often cited as a point of inspiration. Speetjens bridges
these confluences here, in a piece that is planar in design,
but three-dimensionally active in space. —RS

Speetjens uses the wind generated by opening and
closing the tight-fitting drawers to produce musical notes
through the accordion reeds mounted on the back of the
case. Each drawer plays a different note, as if snoring
or wheezing. —JK

(left) Chest of Drawers
Forest Dickey, San Diego, CA
Reclaimed pine and oak barn timbers, steel
84" x 12" x 12"

This piece investigates an aesthetic of urban and
rural tension through the juxtaposition of reclaimed
architectural elements and changes in scale. The recycled
pine timbers are manipulated and reused to layer
associations of architecture and furniture for the viewer.
This relationship creates a unique interaction between
forms of buildings we are familiar with, the materials they
are constructed of, and the objects that inhabit them.
—Forest Dickey

The graphic quality of the steel drawer fronts against
the reclaimed pine adds a beautiful visual rhythm to
the piece. —RS

It's not immediately apparent that most of these little
drawers go right through the timber, encouraging
engagement with the piece from all four sides. It's not
immediately apparent what you would put in this tower
of tiny drawers, your button collection or your colored
pencils perhaps. —JK

Strip Quilt Cupboard
Jim Rose, Kolbert, WI
Found steel with natural rust patina and paint
32.5" x 45" x 21"

Deeply influenced by traditional quilting and its utilitarian and parsimonious use of fabric remnants, this piece translates folk traditions and graphic legacy into the satisfyingly sympathetic and contemporary medium of steel. The piecing of rusted, pitted scrap metals inspired a design of blocks and grids to create a piece of furniture whose design blithely complements its purpose. —*Jim Rose*

Hard materials add irony to a piece that is based on textile tradition. The pieced-together quilt idea uses the beautiful wood grain pattern to mimic textile patterns. —*RS*

(right) End Table Crank Box
Isaac Arms, Bozeman, MT
Fir, maple, steel, and paint
27" x 14" x 14"

Furniture is an interactive medium. We push, pull, turn, and in this case crank in order to access interior spaces. Engaging in these subtle actions is a meditative process that awakens our senses to the importance of not only the furniture but also the object that is kept securely inside. —*Isaac Arms*

A piece with drawers is inherently interactive, but Arms extends the interactivity with a novel way to activate the access to the storage area. —*RS*

Working the crank is easy and crisp. There's no slop in this very satisfying mechanism. —*JK*

(right) 46 Drawer Chest
Jason Howard, Atlanta, GA
Cherry, poplar
72" x 20" x 20"

The chest has 46 drawers, which are in 23 different sizes with 986 parts, 368 dovetails, and it took 440 hours to complete. The whole structure was bolted together and turned to achieve its final shape—an exciting experiment in itself. —*Jason Howard*

Because of the monumental closed cone, the piece takes on an entirely new character as the drawers are opened, highlighting the spiral embedded in the cone. —*RS*

The conical tower sits on a rounded base that is loosely bolted to the floor, allowing it to sway and pivot gently and more than somewhat disconcertingly. The drawers all fit perfectly in their openings; however, in order to maintain the smooth integrity of the form, both drawers and case openings have sharp edges and corners. The drawers get smaller the farther down the cone form you go. —*JK*

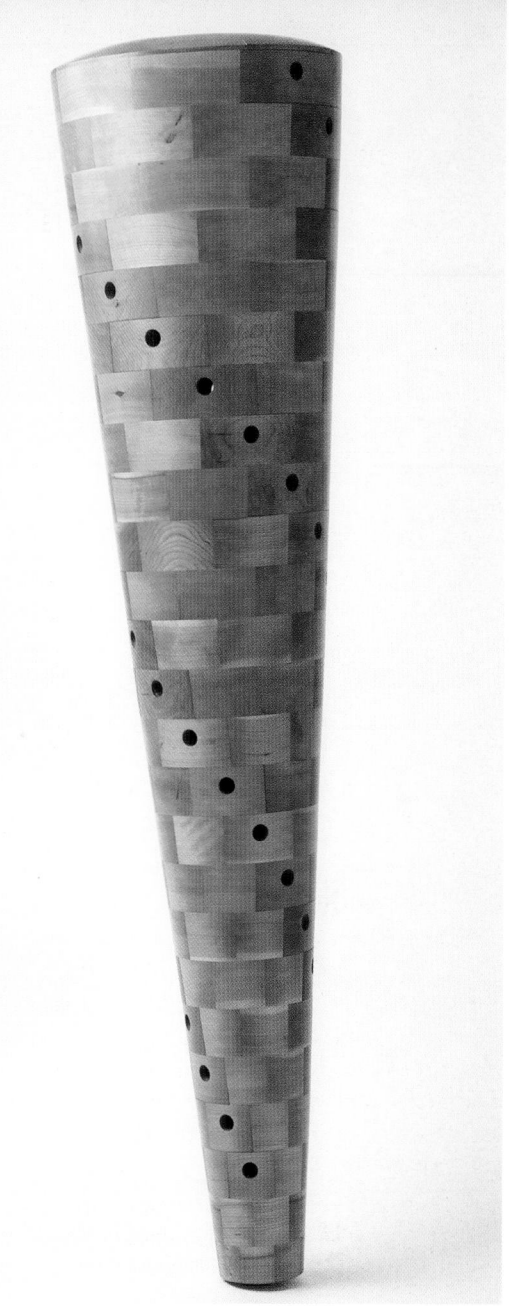

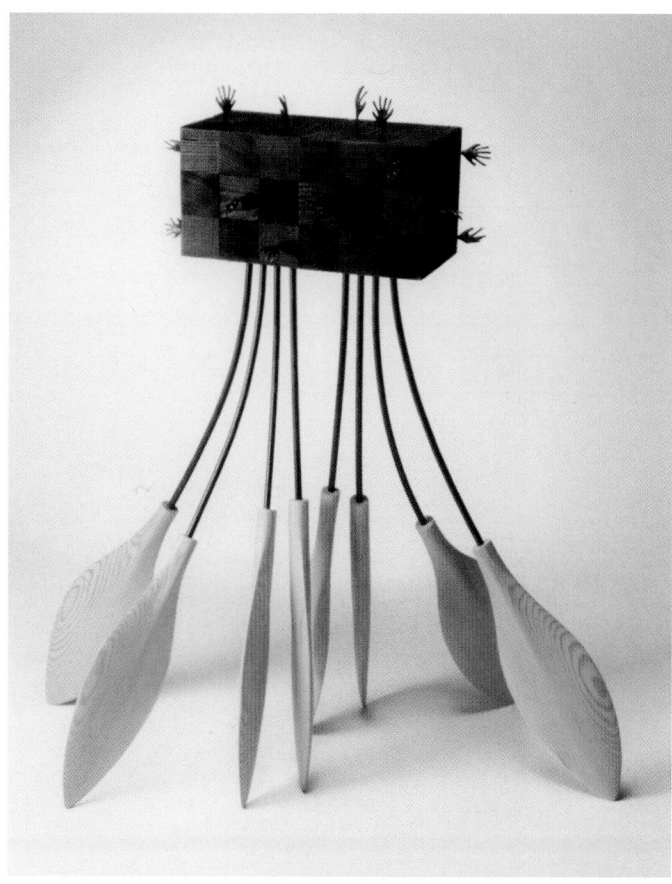

River of Love... or Tears
Jack Larimore, Philadelphia, PA
Ash, Douglas fir, steel, bronze
48" x 44" x 22"

(left) This piece was born out of sadness and frustration with the events on and following September 11, 2001. The only way for me to work my way through this time was to try to find a larger, longer view of life. This piece represents hope and determination for me, relying on the metaphor of a river journey for life. There are four small drawers that suggest the significance of what one might take along, questioning what might be essential. —*Jack Larimore*

Using dramatic contrasts in color, form, and scale, Larimore evokes the many conflicted feelings that remain in our culture over an event that changed our history and the way that we live. —*RS*

The four vestigial drawers fit very tightly in their openings, making them not so easy to find. The cast bronze hands have six fingers each. The charred and ebonized surface is somber and heavy. —*JK*

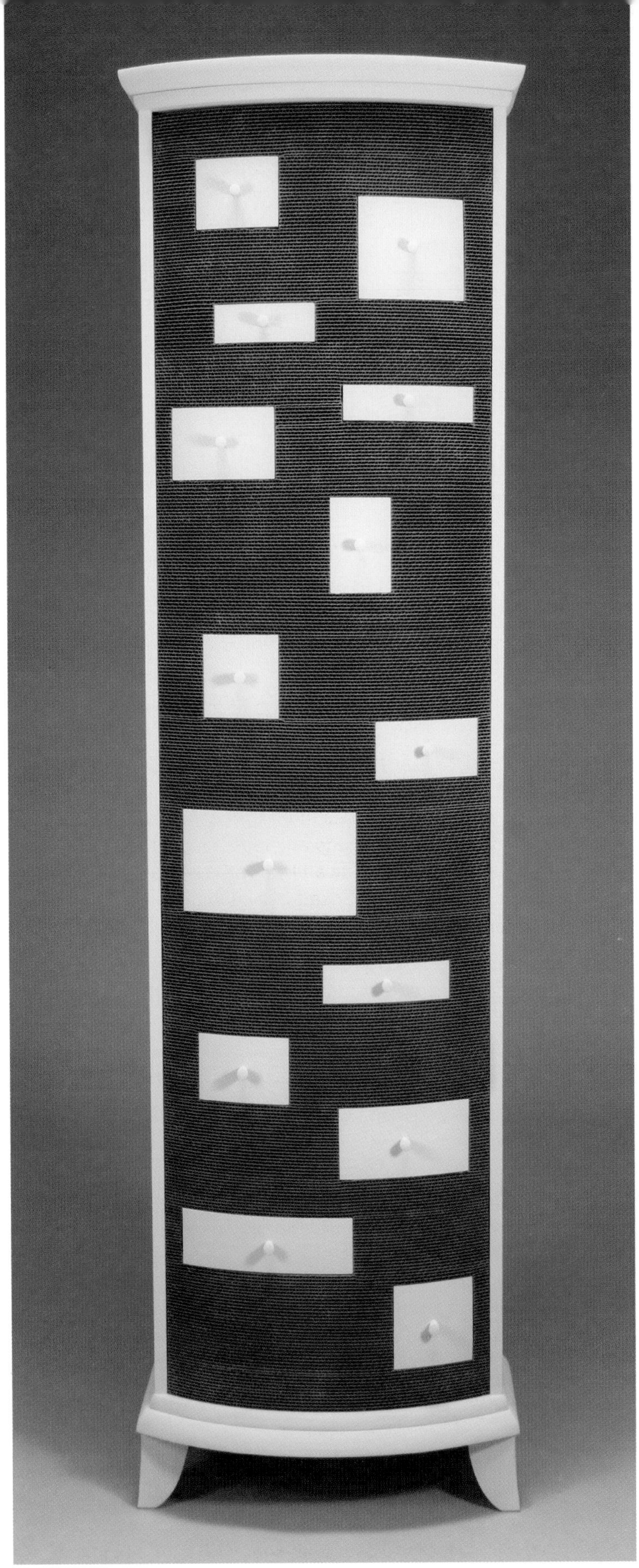

Tall Chest
Jason Schneider, Snowmass Village, CO
Cardboard, ash, milk paint, gold leaf
70" x 17" x 13"

The carcass of this tall chest is made from laminated layers of cardboard. Voids were cut out of the cardboard to accommodate piston-fit drawers. Elevating the status of cardboard from a commonly overlooked and discarded material to a precious material used in furniture offers the viewer a new perspective on its potential use and beauty.
—*Jason Schneider*

By combining materials such as gold leaf, ash, and cardboard in one piece, Schneider asks us to question our material assumptions, and see materials for their inherent possibilities rather than their raw material value. —*RS*

We've seen cardboard furniture before but this piece introduces a delightful glimpse right through the apparently solid material. The corrugations are open enough to show light and motion occurring behind the case. —*JK*

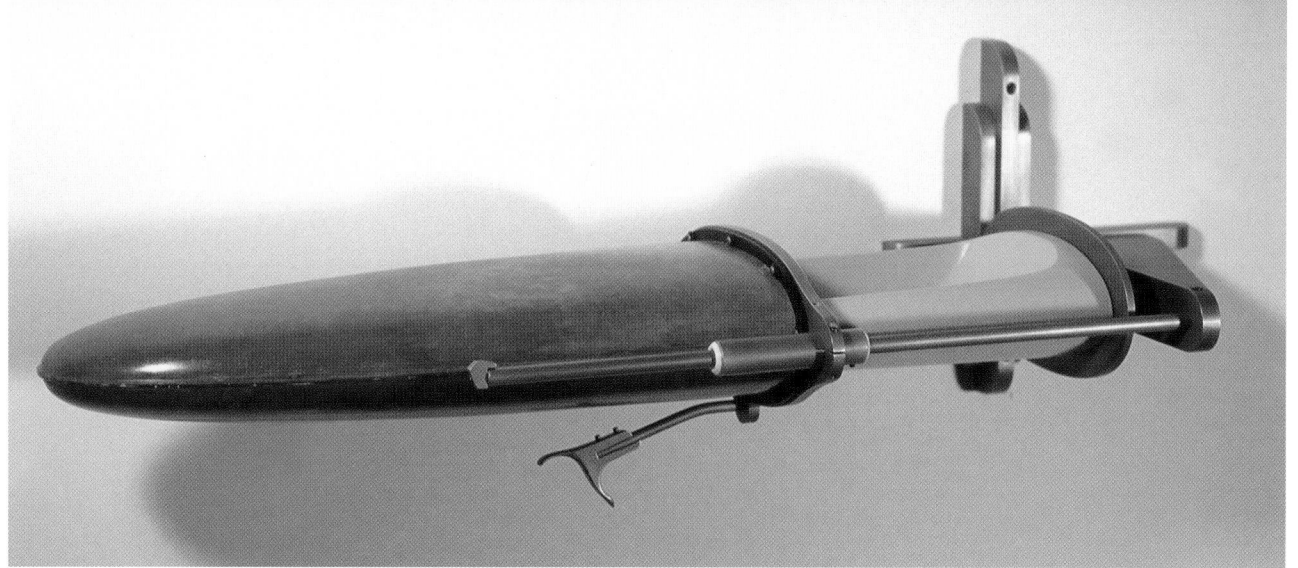

(above) Pod
Todd Partridge, San Diego, CA
Fiberglass, aluminum, wood
12" x 36" x 14"

This object challenges the typical carcass/drawer relationship. Where it is common for the drawer to be the active member of this relationship, *Pod* reverses the role. The drawer is stationary and the carcass moves. The form and aesthetic is derived from my investigation of organic and mechanical devices. *—Todd Partridge*

This piece exemplifies thinking that starts from the core notions of storage and revealing, and uses industrial materials in an innovatively engineered combination to surprise the viewer and enhance the interactive experience. *—RS*

The action is smooth and crisp, with no slop. The translucent fiberglass has a texture reminiscent of leather. *—JK*

(left) Flora Dansu
Brian Pietrowski, Portland, OR
Concrete, steel, ash
52" x 23" x 23"

This piece is based on the tansu furniture of Japan. The design was born out of my great appreciation for the balance of aesthetics and functionality of those Far Eastern case pieces. *—Brian Pietrowski*

Unexpected material choices help the viewer to experience forms based on tradition, but expressed in contemporary language. *—RS*

First you work the key to operate a heavy sliding gate, giving access to a large drawer with a lid that lifts to reveal three smaller drawers. It feels as if it might go on this way forever, drawers within drawers within drawers. *—JK*

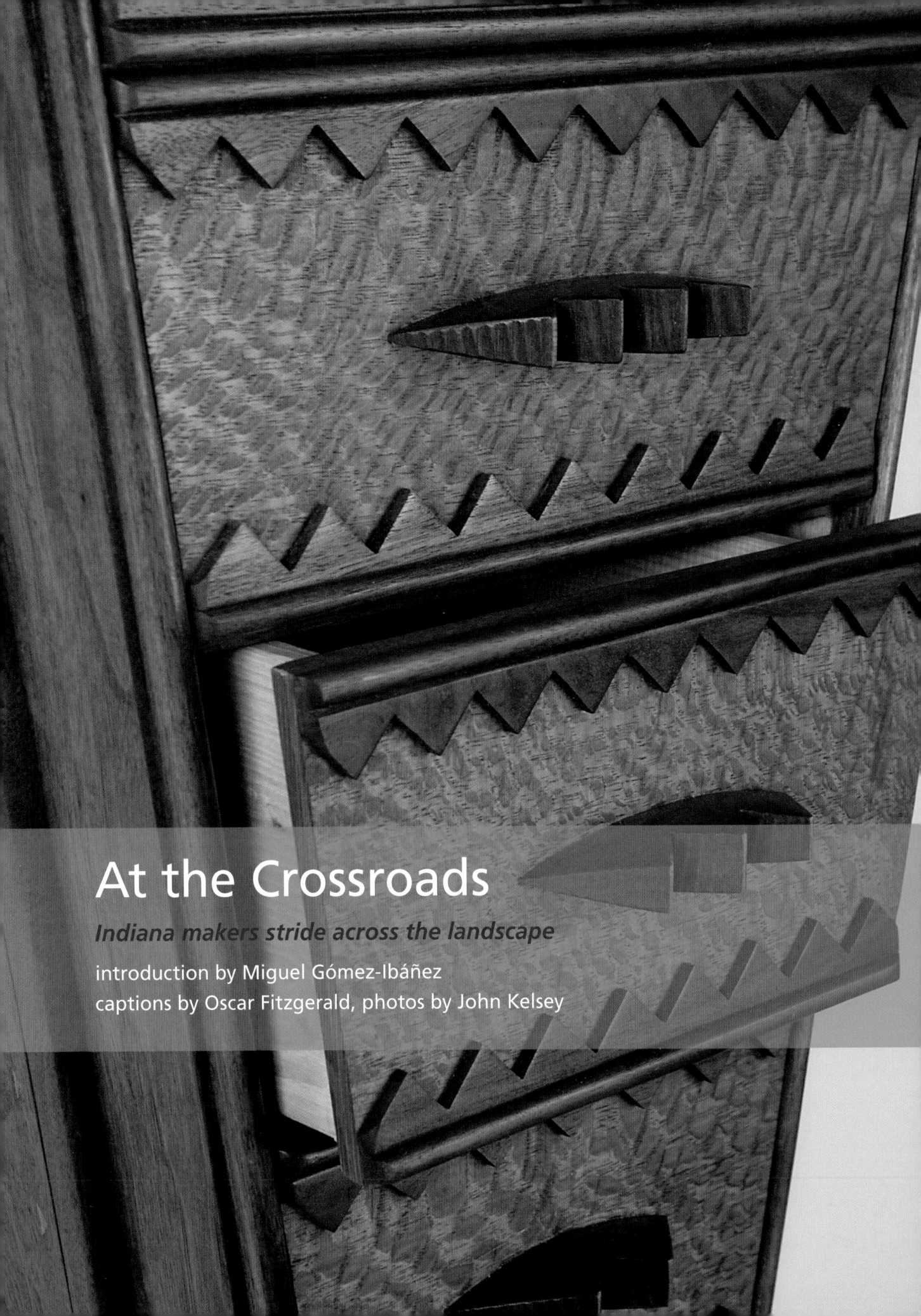

At the Crossroads

Indiana makers stride across the landscape

introduction by Miguel Gómez-Ibáñez
captions by Oscar Fitzgerald, photos by John Kelsey

The annual Furniture Society conference provides an opportunity to get a closer look at the furniture that is being made and sold by makers in the conference region. The 2006 conference exhibition in Indianapolis provided just such a glimpse, featuring a dozen Indiana furniture makers, most with ties to the host institution, the Herron School of Art and Design.

I was eager to find signs of regionalism in the work. We are in the Midwest, after all, so where are the cornfields? Apparently they are here: two of the makers, Cory Robinson (*Terrain*) and Chris Bowman (*Torii #4* and *#5*), include striations in the surfaces of their work that they say are inspired by the furrowed agricultural geography of the region and another, Nick Hollibaugh, whose sculptural wall pieces are not shown, is inspired by farm buildings. Phil Tennant's chair-like sculptures evoke the farm windmills that dot the landscape, and the stretcher beneath his *Sideboard* resembles straight-running railroad tracks. But beyond those literal connections, there are other common themes, notably an interest in layered, painted surfaces, and surfaces that reveal themselves through abrasion or use. Robert Brandt's *Wall Cabinet*, Chris Bowman's *Torii* series, Kenton Hall's *Straddle Stool* and Cory Robinson's *Terrain Cabinet* all feature surface treatments of multiple layers and multiple colors.

The V Box (2005)
John McNaughton, Evansville, IN
Lacewood, walnut, ash
80" H x 16" D x 16" W

McNaughton made this cabinet just after he retired from teaching at the University of Southern Indiana. Of his 50 or so cabinets that are tall and thin, this one is the first in an X shape, a design inspired by Microsoft's Xbox video game player. The trim is local walnut and the case is solid lacewood to which he has applied a walnut stain. He got the idea for the finish after a trip to Mexico where he saw old 18th and 19th century furniture with a light brown patina. Staining the lacewood imparted just the right mellow leathery look. The cornice gave him the most challenge, until he hit upon the idea of laying the saw-tooth molding on its side. The front cornice is freestanding, much like false store fronts in old western towns. The center of the piece, which McNaughton originally designed plain, also presented challenges. The addition of hand shaped, half-round, and V moldings, plus two strips of light-colored lacewood against the dark walnut, eventually provided a nice focal point.

The locally harvested ash drawer sides are joined to the lacewood fronts with finger joints cut on a table saw, a technique McNaughton learned from Tage Frid in a workshop at Penland in North Carolina. The drawers run on a slot in the center of the drawer dividers. He cut the first drawer pull with a band saw that turned out to have a bad blade and a definite wobble that scored the wood. He almost threw the blade away, but decided he liked the effect, and the blade held up until he was able to cut all the pulls. Although he intended the cabinet for his wife, it sold immediately. He has the pictures and the memories, and plans to make another.

Bowman's and Hall's pieces also illustrate a second recurring theme in the exhibition: a fascination with Chinese and Japanese ideas and forms. Along with Phil Tennant's *Sideboard*, Ryan Pfrommer's *Writing Table*, and Tom Tedrow's *Myers Cabinet*, much of the work in this show takes a decidedly Asian stance.

But generalities can't be applied to all of the work. James David Lee approaches his pieces with a very personal touch added to a rigorous engineering intelligence that stands apart in the show. Robert Kasnak's *Desk and Chair* stand alone in their reliance upon traditional furniture forms and the exposition of figured wood. John McNaughton's *V Box* is vintage McNaughton: the idiosyncratic work of a prolific artist who has traveled down many roads during a long career.

It is hard to resist the urge to draw out common themes that will support the idea of regionalism in the work of furniture makers, and an exhibit of makers from a single Midwestern state is a tempting target. But in the end the work does not support the thesis that regionalism is alive and well. Perhaps that is why the exhibit, and the conference as a whole, used the idea of "Crossroads" as its theme. As the name implies, Indiana—and perhaps the Herron School of Art and Design even more so— is a gathering place, a stop along the way for people and ideas traveling across the country. People pass through. Some stay. All are enriched by the confluence.

Miguel Gómez-Ibáñez is past president of The Furniture Society, director of the North Bennet Street School in Boston, and a furniture maker.

Oscar Fitzgerald is a faculty member at the Smithsonian Institution/Corcoran School of Art and Design master's program in the decorative arts.

Mirror (2004)
James David Lee, Indianapolis, IN
Sugar pine, glass
60" H x 37" W

Lee bought a window sash just for the old glass at the Brimfield Antique Show in Massachusetts, but then saw other possibilities for re-engineering it into a mirror. He likes the idea of finding things and making them into something else. He laminated the edges of the frame to give them a taper, then used an engraver to laboriously cut striations on the edges, and finally applied gold and silver leaf to the frame. He added a cornice of sugar pine with vertical striations, which he cut with a router. The sugar pine strip at the bottom of the mirror holds test tubes in holes fitted with rubber O-rings, which he got from his wife, a clinical research scientist. Sandwiched between two sheets of glass at the bottom and the top of the frame are 88 vials containing chilies that his wife received from a doctor friend during a trip to Santa Fe, New Mexico. The back of the mirror, which stands about five feet high, comes off easily so that he can change the contents of the vials. Lee's daughter is an oboist, and he is thinking about replacing the chilies with spent oboe reeds. This is his first mirror, but he hopes do more. He likes the way it makes a personal family statement.

Vanity (2006)
James David Lee, Indianapolis, IN
Maple, glass, aluminum
76" H x 54" W x 34" D

Lee, the shop master for the Furniture Design Department's wood shop at the Herron School of Art and Design, made this double vanity for his own use. The eight-inch aluminum sheets and U-channel came from an audio rack he found at an auction. Bird's-eye maple veneer outlines the drawer dividers and the frames that house the mirrors while solid, curly maple strips edge the top surface. The central mirror comes all the way down to the glass surface and rests on two aluminum tabs at the base. All the mirrors fit into grooves cut into the wood frames behind the aluminum U-channel, which has been split. Lee textured the edges of the grooves in the wood with a pencil; when reflected in the mirror, this creates the illusion that the aluminum strips framing the mirrors are half an inch thick. Lee attached all the legs to the frame with difficult tri-miters, cutting mortise-and-tenon joints on the 45-degree surfaces.

The central drawer pulls out to reveal a U-shaped drawer so that the drawer does not cover up the mirror-bottomed shadow box set into the glass-covered surface. If a person sits on one side of the double vanity, that person's face and body is reflected into the mirror of the shadow box. The surprise is that while a person sitting on the other side will also see her own face in the shadow box, it will be attached to the body of the other person.

Writing Table (2004)
Ryan Pfrommer, Providence, RI
Spalted maple, cherry
32" H x 29" W x 20" D

Pfrommer made this table as a student at the Herron School of Art and Design after spending a summer in China. The table was inspired by historical furniture he saw in Hunan Province while studying with art students there.
The two back legs are screwed to a medial stretcher and doweled into the three-piece, glued-up, spalted maple top. The cherry legs and front skirt are hand shaped. It took five or six wooden models to get the right curves. The entire piece was finished with Danish oil. Pfrommer is now a graduate student at the Rhode Island School of Design, and his work has taken a completely different turn.

Terrain Cabinet (2006)
Cory Robinson, Indianapolis, IN
Ash, maple, poplar, mahogany
48" H x 20" W x 14" D

A graduate of the Herron School of Art and Design, Robinson went on to get his MFA from San Diego State and is now an assistant professor of furniture design at Herron. The cabinet on frame recalls the signature pieces by James Krenov, but instead of highlighting the grain of the wood as Krenov does, Robinson has built his piece around the complex, router-carved surface of the poplar doors. They suggest tilled earth or landscape patterns viewed from the air, hence the title, *Terrain*. The maple biscuit-joined cabinet sits on laminated ash legs that gently taper from top to bottom, flare out at the base, and rest on adjustable brass feet. These facilitate leveling and raise the piece ever so slightly off the floor to make it look like it is floating. The cabinet also floats off the base, supported by four brass tubes set back from each corner through which bolts pass. Robinson cut out the poplar crosspiece freehand on a band saw, leaving the saw marks to give it a log-like texture similar to the legs he uses for his benches.

The doors are stained black; the beveled edge around the case is painted a metallic green; the interior shelves in a crosshair pattern are finished with red milk paint, and the dovetailed mahogany drawer fronts with turned ebony pulls are left natural. The base is also stained black, but then sanded and rubbed with graphite powder to give it a burnished metallic look. The piece is lacquered, first with a coat mixed with graphite and then a clear coat. Although he usually works from sketches, Robinson built a full-scale mockup for this to get the proportions just right. It was made for sale and was shown at the Function + Art gallery in Chicago.

Wall Cabinet (2006)
Robert Brandt, Notre Dame, IN
Mahogany, 30" H x 15.5" W x 8.25" D

Brandt teaches furniture design in the School of Architecture, University of Notre Dame. He came to the school in 1992 at the behest of the department head, Thomas Gordon Smith, who wanted to introduce a furniture program to complement his own emphasis on classical architecture. The carving on the front of the cabinet, one of a series of four he has made, is based on Medieval Gothic linenfold carving, while the sides are patterned after traditional Gothic cathedral windows that he found in period pattern books. Originally, he built a crenellated cornice with turrets for the crest but felt it did not blend well with the rest of the cabinet. This cornice, with simple, classical Doric moldings, seemed to unify the piece, even if based on a different design vocabulary. The surface was worked with layers of acrylic paint, stain, and dyes that were rubbed, sanded, and aged with a heat gun to attain an antique finish. Gold acrylic paint, which he washed with another coat of green and black paint and also subjected to a heat gun, sets off the linenfold carving. With this technique, if Brandt does not like the effect, it is easy to sand down the finish and start over, in contrast to the unforgiving French polish he often applies to his furniture. He even roughed-up the stock brass hinges and knob and soaked them in aniline dye to give them an antique look as well. Although the cabinet appears to sit on a shelf in the manner of cabinets he saw illustrated in Thomas Hope's early 19th century design book, *Household Furniture and Interior Decoration*, in reality it hangs from cleats attached to the back and the wall.

(facing page) Torii #4, Torii #5 (2006)
Chris Bowman, Indianapolis, IN
Cherry, poplar
25" H x 26.5" W x 10.5" D

The name for these tables derives from the curved shapes of the cherry tops that recall Japanese *torii* or gates at the entrances to temples that Bowman saw in books illustrating Japanese architecture. A full-time furniture maker and 2000 graduate of the Herron School of Art and Design, Bowman has made six of these tables in the past two years, each slightly different. He achieved the elliptical shape by forming bendable plywood around plywood ribs. About half the work was in the finishing of the façades. First, he cut closely spaced lines across the surface with a V chisel, imparting a corduroy-like appearance. Growing up in Martinsville, Indiana, south of Indianapolis in farm country, he was surrounded by row upon row of corn. The chiseled lines recall that childhood image. Then he applied up to eight coats of red milk paint as a ground, and an equal number of finish coats that he wiped down with a wet cloth to expose, ever so faintly, the red undercoat. A final rubbing with steel wool imparted a sheen, which he preserved with a Sam Maloof oil finish: polyurethane and linseed oil.

The single drawer that slides through the center of each base can be accessed from either side. He shaped the projecting drawer fronts with a Surform rasp, leaving the marks of the tool to provide added texture. The drawers were band-sawn out of a single piece of poplar in the manner of the trademark drawers by Art Carpenter.

Table (2006)
Phil Tennant, Indianapolis, IN
Bubinga, wenge, ebonized mahogany
34" H x 120" W x 24" D

Tennant made this table as a commission for a specific place in a long and narrow
hall. The three *Throne* chairs are displayed on the wall above it. In contrast to his chair
sculptures, where he starts with a rough sketch and invents as he goes along, this
table with all its complex joinery had to be designed precisely before he could begin
construction. The grid form with exposed and interlocking elements is his signature
style, which he has been refining for the past 15 years. Over time Tennant has simplified
his work by editing out and cutting back on the number of elements, making the
structure stronger and better engineered, and the joinery more precise. His first table
with a granite top actually wobbled when people walked by it.

The inspiration for the furniture derives clearly from the Arts and Crafts movement, the
work of Charles Rennie Mackintosh, and particularly Japanese architecture. Although
Tennant has never visited Japan, he has assiduously studied Japanese design through
books, notably temples and the structures used to hold giant gongs. His work is an
exercise in balance, form, and structure.

Throne A, B and C (2004)
Phil Tennant, Indianapolis, IN
Wenge, bubinga, ebony, bronze rod
36" H x 7" W x 5" D

Tennant, head of the furniture design department in the Heron School of Art and Design, finds these chairs—really wall sculptures that he can turn out spontaneously in a couple of days—a nice respite from his more exacting and labor-intensive furniture. The reddish bubinga and the darker wenge elements that make up the chairs are carefully joined and pegged together. The legs on one are lashed together top and bottom with waxed linen thread that might be found on a fishing pole. He likes the chair form because it evokes a ceremonial throne or a place for special people to sit. The chairs serve as a metaphor for the people who might use them. One has masculine connotations with arrows for hunting, while another has a soft feminine connotation with the rounded crest rails and gentle curves on the pendulum. The open seats suggest people of no substance. Tennant particularly likes to use plumb bobs, repeating them on all these chairs to represent being centered or balanced and how fragile that state is. In the feminine chair the plumb bob is centered in a position of perfection. In others it is off center to imply a change in direction. In the end, these chairs are about form and shape and invite multiple interpretations.

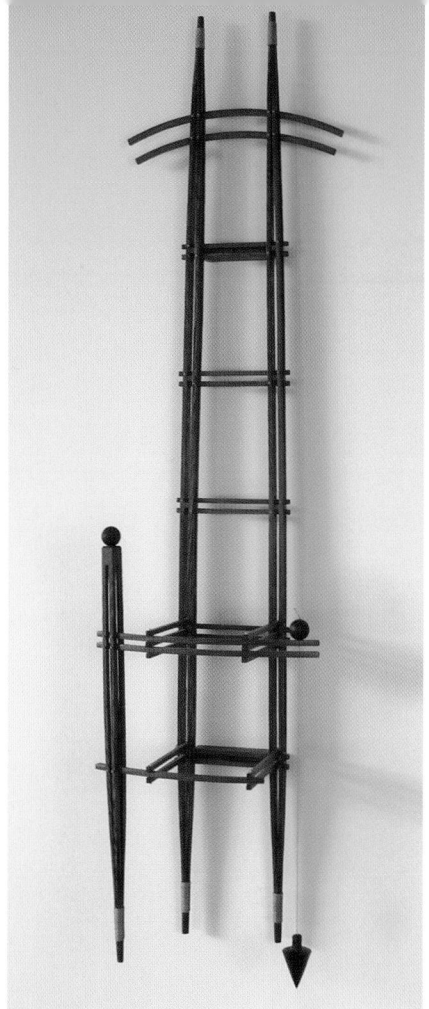

Straddle Stool (2006)
Kenton Hall, Muncie, IN
Maple, white oak
32" H x 12" W x 15" D

A graduate of the Rhode Island School of Design with an MFA in furniture design, Hall now teaches at Ball State University in Muncie, Indiana. Since he was in graduate school in 1985 he has used all sorts of woods, from walnut to redwood salvaged from an old water tower, to make runs of these stools, usually in sets of two or four, plus enough extra parts to allow for one reject. They have become his signature piece. Hall once rode Raleigh bikes so he has contoured the seat like a bicycle seat, and the crosspiece, which actually reminds him of an English shovel handle, acts like a handlebar. Less obvious is the influence of Chinese joinery. The tenons at the back of the maple seat and the top of the oak back leg have 45-degree mitered shoulders that fit into corresponding V-cuts and are secured with pegs. The turned oak front legs are tenoned through the seat and wedged in the typical Windsor chair manner. To maintain the correct angle for the legs, which was traditionally done by eye, Hall instead planes the underside corners of the seat to the same angle at which he then drills the holes for the legs. The whole stool is finished off with a fine rasp to give it a texture that avoids the need to sand. Finally, Hall paints it with milk paint, in this case black, then red, and then a final coat of green. Not at all uncomfortable, the chair is designed to be straddled so that the sitter's arms rest on the crosspiece.

Myers Cabinet (1998)
R. Thomas Tedrowe, Jr., Columbus, IN
Mahogany, makore, ebony, black coral
69" H x 22" W x 13" D

With a BFA in sculpture from the Herron School of Art and Design and an MFA in furniture design from the Rhode Island School of Design, Tedrowe has been a full-time furniture maker since the early 1980s. The Myerses wanted a piece of Tedrowe furniture so he proposed this design, and they loved it. The cabinet is human-scaled with Art Deco influences. The ebonized mahogany legs, cut on a band saw and hand shaped with a spokeshave, show the influence of the French Art Deco artists Jacques Emile Ruhlmann and Eugene Printz. The legs are joined to the base that is filled with sand to stabilize the piece. While traveling in Mexico Tedrowe found black coral in a jeweler's shop, and used the material for the door pulls, which he fastened to ebony posts with silver wire to give the design an oriental flavor. The exterior of the cabinet is veneered with figured makore, often called African cherry, from the Ivory Coast, and the inside, fitted with two drawers and a shelf, is curly maple. Each interior drawer has a secret compartment beneath a false bottom. One of the drawers that pulls out from the side of the cabinet has yet another secret space at the back of the drawer. The fronts of these drawers in the base have mitered ends and are joined to the sides with sliding dovetails, a technique he learned from Tage Frid at RISD. It took a couple of months to make the cabinet, with most of the time spent applying the veneers, particularly over the ogee curved surfaces on the top.

Robert Kasnak,
Brownsburg, IN

Desk (2002)
Figured maple
and ebony
45" H x 43.5" W
x 27.5" D

Chair (2003)
Figured maple
and ebony
35" H x 26.5" W
x 27.5" D

Kasnak runs a successful antique restoration business and occasionally makes custom furniture. Both the desk and chair, which he made for his own use, won the Governor's Choice award as best in show at the Indianapolis craft fair and were on display at the Governor's Mansion in a group show for three months. He has combined highly figured tiger and bird's-eye maple with rare maple where bark has become embedded in the annual rings. This bark-inclusion maple provides a focal point for the doors on the desk and the splats of the chair. The influence of Charles and Henry Greene, the Arts and Crafts architects who worked in California in the early 20th century, is readily apparent. The ebony inlay on the desk and chair legs, the skirts, the back slats of the chair and on the chair arms stands proud of the surface, as do the subtly rounded finger joints on the top and bottom of the desk compartment and the breadboard ends of the writing surface. All the edges of the desk are rounded, even the subtly shaped ebony and maple pulls. Kasnak has employed the theme of threes in the three shelves, the shaping of the shelf edges, the stepped-back document compartments, the three slats on the chair, and the shaping of the front edge of the chair arms. The inlaid ebony flowers on the chair slats recall the stylized flowers on Charles Rennie Mackintosh furniture in Glasgow, Scotland, at the turn of the century, and on a Gustav Stickley desk designed by Harvey Ellis in 1904.

Robert Kuo
Fluted Entry Table
Repoussé copper
30" H x 42" Dia.

Craft and the Designer

What is the value of craftsmanship in manufactured furniture?

by Robert Griffith

When considering the value of furniture, most people would agree that well-crafted furniture offers higher value than designed products that do not reveal craft values. If this is true, then what can be said for furniture that clearly displays a craft process or look? For this discussion, we must recognize that a craft aesthetic and culture exists, and also that designers who make a significant case for craft may nonetheless operate completely outside of this craft culture. The studio craft practitioner (or studio designer) represents a kind of bridge between the culture of craft and the practice of product design.

Some may argue that the role of craft in industrial design has diminished in recent times, giving way to style or, in the worst case, novelty. Contrary to this view, studio designers and new venues for the production and sale of their work have emerged. The tradition of handwork, which continues in pockets of offshore cultures, provides opportunities for the manufacture of luxury goods with a high craft component. The marketplace increasingly recognizes the value of handwork and craft in such products.

Any consideration of the value of craft would benefit from distinguishing between the "collector" and the "consumer." To the collector, the quality and provenance of the craft object is paramount, whereas to the consumer, quality is one of a number of highly valued considerations in the acquisition of goods; other considerations would include price, color, availability, and delivery time. It is additionally useful to distinguish between furniture and other goods in analyzing and evaluating the components of value. What can be said in support of craft in furniture production may be applied to other industries; however, it is important to recognize that the jewelry and garment industries (for example) operate within completely different parameters for production and sales, not to mention the creation and development of products.

Robert Kuo: Craft in collaboration with industry

Designers who engage craftsmen in collaboration with industry may reflect a craft aesthetic. Such designers may find a home with companies that support special or limited editions. Robert Kuo's collections for McGuire, for example, distinguish this designer and support the case for handwork as

Robert Kuo

value-adding luxury. This studio designer's work is heavily influenced by Chinese furniture tradition and culture, as well as by the craft skills available to him in Chinese workshops. Kuo explains, "I work with artisans who have the traditional skills but since my designs are the way they are, it is pushing the boundaries of what they are accustomed to."[1] In addition to the designer's collaboration with McGuire, Kuo's California-based studio develops and markets furniture products that are available directly from the designer's studio. Kuo's work represents a diverse form of craft practice for American furniture companies.

Kuo, whose craft training originated in the cloisonné studio of his father, marries traditional

Robert Griffith: Atelier

My own design practice has reaffirmed my instincts and intuition regarding creativity and the assigned value of craft. My education in the business began in 1997 with gallery and museum shows of one-of-a-kind furniture. In 2001 I founded my own design and product development company with my industry partner, Kent Harris. In 2002, we were able to introduce The Atelier Collection *at Highpoint International Furniture market.*
The collection reflected the craft aesthetic I had practiced and presented over the previous thirty years. The designs themselves emerged in a fluid and natural continuum. Learning the business and knowing which business I was in, however, was an entirely different matter.

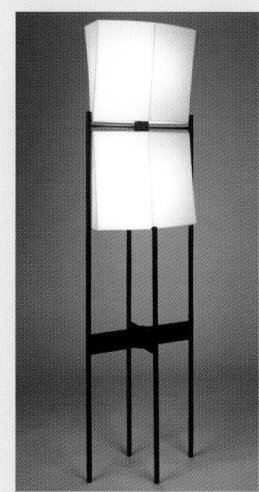

Robert Griffith
Caress Light
Tubular steel, paper
72" H x 20" W x 12" D
Photo: Lisa Hinkle

Part of my strategy is to design products based on the existing capabilities of the staff and physical plant of the companies I am associated with. This streamlined the design process, with prototypes initially being built through my partner's fabrication business. I was fortunate to find partners in industry who were eager to adapt my craft aesthetic and to develop new strategies for marketing the work. My background as a metalsmith and artist contributed greatly to developing products with manufacturing personnel. Successful partnerships can offer sharing of responsibilities as well as a sounding board for ideas.

In the beginning, less than 10% of my time had anything to do with creativity. This can be a pitfall for any designer. It has taken determination and discipline to find the balance between keeping the train on track and focusing on where it is headed. Knowing what is required to support the production of designs is always an issue. Questions arise: What are the risks? Will I be satisfied with the level of control over my designs in exchange for royalties? Am I best suited to determining my own place and level of production?

It has been important to me to be as aware as possible, to be curious as a creative person, and to employ a paradigm based on inquiry. Being informed and in touch is paramount.

Robert Griffith is a studio designer and professor of art at Marywood University in Pennsylvania.

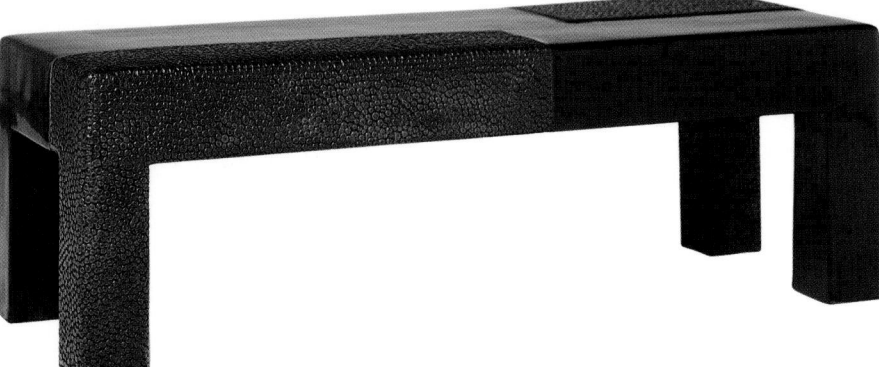

Robert Kuo

left: Pebble Bench Table
Black lacquer and copper
repoussé on wood
50″ W x 18″ D x 16″ H

below: Cloud Small Cabinet
Carved wood, lacquer
27″ H x 32″ W x 22″ D

technique to a highly refined aesthetic. His aesthetic is supported by production at independent studios in China. "I design the pieces and assign the different studios the work. Different studios have different specialties. One studio is very good at the leaf design, another one does all of the fluted design, another works with the wood grain design. The more familiar the studio is with the design, the faster and more consistent the work." Working this way, Kuo finds that the design process can be long and difficult. "I don't design with other people. Sometimes it takes one and a half years before a first piece is completed because it is a process. Either technical issues or a design issue, the development process is long." By working the way he does, Kuo pays homage to Chinese culture through masterfully crafted individual pieces and is helping to keep centuries-old craft practice alive. This is, in fact, a mission for Kuo, whose familiarity and expertise with antiquities provides direction and meaning for the work. Kuo's work challenges

our perceptions of China as a monolithic manufacturing giant.

In Kuo's case, products involving coats of lacquer applied over a period up to 32 weeks present new considerations for the value of craft and its contribution to the end product. These products are very much the outcome of the designer's own studio practice. The cloisonné enameling, repoussé, and lacquer work involved in the production of Kuo designs demonstrate the value of craft through sophisticated form and finish. For Robert Kuo, handwork is the "ultimate luxury."

Hans Wegner: Industrialized craftsmanship

The influence of the Chinese furniture-making tradition is not limited to Chinese designers. Hans Wegner, the well-known mid-century Scandinavian designer, demonstrated an appreciation for Chinese antiquities through his designs of the 1940s and 50s, notably *The Chinese Chair (No. 1)* of 1940. Wegner, who began his career as a carpenter's apprentice, went on to work with Danish furniture companies who manufactured and marketed his designs on a royalty basis. Later in life, Wegner's designs would come to define the "modern chair." *The Chinese Chair* greatly

Hans Wegner

influenced Wegner's *Wishbone Chair*, developed in 1950, and to this day is continued in production by Carl Hansen & Son in Denmark.

In 1950, Wegner's *Round Chair*, featured on the cover of *Interiors* magazine, not only contributed to his fame but also helped to define what we now know as "Danish Design." Of the five companies that produced Wegner designs in the mid-1950s, Carl Hansen & Son is now the principal manufacturer of selected designs. The company has manufactured vintage Wegner designs for half a century, including the *Elbow Chair*, next page, recently re-introduced at the International Contemporary Furniture Fair in New York. Wegner's designs, which demonstrate a restraint of design elements and absence of decoration, helped to bring international appreciation for "functionalism as ideology" and later as a "style." Wegner has been quoted as saying, "The best in Danish design is not a style or a fashionable trend but a work method for solving functional problems—with style."[2]

Wegner's genius and creativity emerged through a deliberate analytical process which paired craft with industry. Wegner's understanding of wood technology allowed designs to move forward in

Hans J. Wegner
Three-Legged Chair (1963)
Photo: Soren Hansen

collaboration with the craftsmen in the Hansen workshop. In the Jens Bernsen book on Wegner, the author refers to the process of producing Wegner's designs as "industrialized craftsmanship." With assembly done by hand and attention paid to all the aspects of creating a highly crafted product of quality, the manufacture of Wegner's designs preserves the value of Scandinavian craft, not to mention "style."[2]

Wegner products reflect the designer's reverence for wood: "Love of wood is something that all mankind has in common. Regardless of where people come from, they cannot stop themselves from letting their hands stroke a piece of wood, hold it, sniff it, and experience the material." Like the architect who exposes the bones of a building to be experienced as a design element, Wegner's joinery process is evident in the overall design. The visible joinery emphasizes the craft behind the chair. It implies quality applied by a master craftsperson. Wegner's practice and application of craft contributes greatly to the overall value of the piece. In addition, it provides pedigree and promotes a lineage of craft practice in collaboration with industry.

When properly promoted, the presence of craft practiced in the design and development of furniture products becomes a valuable sales tool. Sales to the consumer have always required an educational process. Furniture companies who

Hans J. Wegner
Y Chair (1950)
Photo: Soren Hansen

Hans J. Wegner
Elbow Chair (1956)
Photo: Soren Hansen

represent work by designers who practice craft recognize that craft is integrated into the product from concept to marketplace: craft is not an element that can be added on. It is a quality issue and one that must be factored into the cost of production, and ultimately, in the price paid by the consumer. After establishing the case for quality and reverence for material, in the example of Hans Wegner and Robert Kuo, a "timelessness" for design emerges. With goals of longevity built into the process of manufacture and presentation to the consumer, these designs present a strong case for the visibility of craft as the hallmark of quality in furniture.

Mid-century Modern

Mid-century furniture, which appears at auction, on the Internet, and in specialty showrooms, offers collectors and interior designers opportunities to acquire important, well-crafted work by iconic 20th-century designers. Gallery showrooms are increasingly presenting Modernist and contemporary furniture in the form of limited editions by designers alongside carefully selected vintage pieces. Gallerie Kreo in Paris deals exclusively with commissioned and limited edition work. In The New York Times's *Style* magazine, design editor Pilar Viladas describes this market as "hotter."[3]

At New York's R Twentieth Century Design the showroom clientele are provided with extraordinary examples of mid-century design through featured exhibitions. These exhibitions are often presented as installations, with furniture and other products in their original environments. The showroom is transformed into a setting that showcases the work in the best possible manner. This venue for design presents work of the well-known, alongside designers who had experienced little recognition in their lifetime. Co-owner Evan Snyderman makes the case for craft in the equation of quality and value. "People want quality now,"[4] Snyderman said. Documentation regarding authenticity, provenance, and the why, when, and where related to the designer is important. Rarity also factors into the price. The research required to provide this service to customers has become a hallmark of the company. But what is striking is that the clientele for vintage and contemporary furniture, according to Snyderman, "is people who are furnishing a home, not necessarily collectors."

"Getting people to believe in what you are doing is part of the challenge. You have to be a chameleon, set trends, and stay ahead of the game," Snyderman explained. The gallery brings the worlds of craft and design together on the same plane to complement each other. Snyderman also notes that "things move more quickly today." Accessibility and delivery time looms large. Agents of design must be poised to respond quickly and effectively to customers. To facilitate this, R Twentieth Century Design holds an inventory and performs restoration (when required) in their Brooklyn warehouse. This form of service to the customer is important in keeping ahead.

In the climate of the post-9/11 marketplace for furnishings designed and created by studio practitioners, collectors of craftwork re-examined their return on investments of all sorts. As expressed by Evan Snyderman, "The community of craft collectors is not regenerating itself.... If the craft world does not embrace the new young collectors, its future does not look good. A time for craft designers to reinvent themselves is at hand. The opportunity for craft to be accepted as a viable form of art and design remains strong."

Wendell Castle: Strategies for keeping the edge sharp

In 2004, R Twentieth Century Design presented "Autoplastic," an exhibition of fiberglass work that designer and artist Wendell Castle created between 1968 and 1973. In 2006 the gallery presented another vintage collection of signed and numbered limited editions entitled the "Wendell Castle Black Edition." Presentations like these help establish the artist in the public eye. The gallery also

Wendell Castle

networks with other galleries in New York to coordinate simultaneous events featuring the same artists. This contributes to the credibility of the work and ultimately its value.

Castle, who is widely recognized for his mastery in wood, has embraced other materials, including plastic and metal, in a continuum of creativity, productivity, and enterprise which began in the early 1960s. In the *Autoplastic* exhibition catalog essay by Donald Albrecht, the artist is credited with the statement that "one must not be subservient to materials—aesthetics should be preeminent."[5] Albrecht describes Castle's *Molar Group* dental shapes "as showing the influence of the early 1970s neo-surrealism." It is this group, consisting of four works, that was "re-introduced" using the original

molds in gloss black by Castle and R Twentieth Century Design. Albrecht additionally quotes Castle: "The significant thing about my work is not what it is made of but what it is."

In addition to producing "one-off" gallery work and signed limited editions, Castle helped found the manufacturing company Icon in 2000. He acknowledges that this endeavor and building the associated collection is a "difficult and complex subject." The Wendell Castle Collection introduced at the International Contemporary Furniture

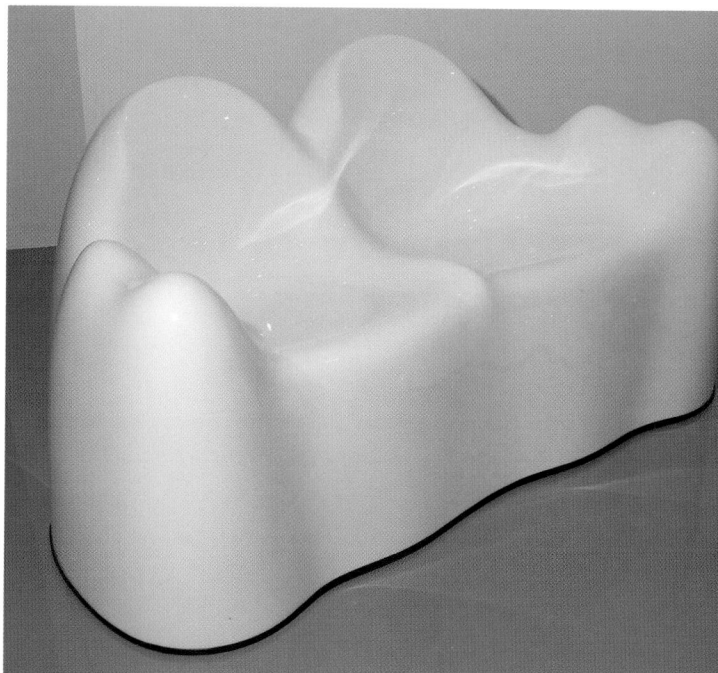

Wendell Castle
Molar Settee

Fair by Icon has taken the path of residential contract furniture primarily targeted to architects and interior designers. Castle explained, "In the contract market you generally don't make anything until it's sold and you don't have to keep inventory."[6] When considering the decision to start the Icon manufacturing facility in Rochester, NY, the ability to have control with the knowledge that the work would be done properly was important to Castle. The marketing side has turned out to be "difficult and expensive," he said. "Now we are trying to get a little more feedback from the showrooms on what people might buy before we go ahead with something." Castle emphasizes custom options offered on wood species and finishes. Delivery remains a factor in having an edge over offshore manufacturers. "Often, delivery time is more important than price. The competitive edge you have is doing custom work and delivering it quickly," Castle said.

Castle's strategy for getting fresh work out and keeping the "edge" sharp acknowledges the need to be involved with the showrooms. "You have to really keep on top of it… you have to visit them

Wendell Castle
Cloud Dining Table

[showrooms]… You have to introduce new things… you have to keep things happening." In this respect, Wendell Castle believes that "fashion and art have a lot in common."

Establishing the value of craft

Design critic James Evans makes a case for the "intelligence of the hand… as too long undervalued in 20th century art making." To Evans, the "language of skill… has been long dismissed and considered an inappropriate strategy to bring to bear in the production of personally expressive works of art."[7] For the studio designer, however, the value of handwork is highly prized by

companies presenting products with the assigned value of quality based on craft. Studio designers might do well to observe industry practice for production and successful retail practice, in order to develop new making and marketing strategies. Any comparison between market-driven design generated by industry with highly crafted and thoughtfully produced work by studio designers could benefit from an accounting of the attributes of both realms. In the example of developing brand identity for companies like Knoll and Herman Miller, artists such as Harry Bertoia (who created the *Diamond Chair* for Knoll) and Isamu Noguchi (whose c. 1950s tables continue to be produced by Herman Miller) provide continued credibility and identity. In these two examples, the stature and reputation of the designers allows the industry to present their designs not as craft, but as fine art.

In an exhibition catalog foreword, museum director Pekka Saarela provides a succinct statement of the case for Finnish craft as practiced by designer Tapio Wirkkala. "This analysis is of equal relevance today, as once again discussion revolves around the relationship between the designer and industry and the added value that craft offers industrial products."[8]

Extraordinary examples of creativity linked to entrepreneurship and industry can be seen in fashion's haute couture. Small-scale fashion studios developed by such designers as Issey Miyake have redefined fashion as art by reinventing the kimono and other traditional Japanese garments. Miyake's approach to fashion is based on experimentation, the craft associated with fabric, and the garments' relationship to the human form. The designer's firsthand knowledge of material and processes offers Miyake a distinct edge. He has been quoted as saying, "I am interested in the space between the body and the clothes so that the body can feel entirely at ease. Because each person's body shape is different, this space creates an

To find out more...

For Robert Griffith's collection, see www.griffithatelier.com.

For Robert Kuo's studio, www.robertkuo.com. For Kuo's production designs marketed through McGuire, www.kohlerinteriors.com.

To see the full range of Hans Wegner furniture in current production, visit www.dmk.dk/designers.

For Wendell Castle's studio furniture, www.wendellcastle.com. For Castle's full range of production designs marketed through Icon, www.wendellcastlecollection.com.

For mid-century Modern furniture, www.r20thcentury.com.

For more about Issey Miyake, (www.isseymiyake.co.jp).

individual form. It also gives the wearer freedom of movement for body and spirit."[9] Some may wonder if any other contemporary designer besides Miyake has more effectively applied a design paradigm responding to the human form.

Japanese design has been described by Helen Rees in *The Culture of Craft* as being "dream-like, allowing the imagination to roam unrestrained." In some cases designers are "given [by companies] time and freedom to develop ideas for designs often with no commercial application."[10] In the West, craft continues to be perceived as a product of culture, while manufacturing is associated with technology. In our time, any attempt to define culture in terms of technology will benefit from the exercise of creativity aligned with enterprise.

For fashion designers like Issey Miyake, "the face of the industry is transformed through the conceptual and creative application of aspects of traditional culture, and embracing new technological developments."

The studio designer is challenged now as ever before to inform and transform the market. Manufacturers and consumers continue to look to designers to set trends and contribute to a sense of connoisseurship. A new appreciation for luxury that craft and handwork represent is in place. This introduces new opportunities to the studio designer, as well as new challenges for those whose creative vision can be aligned with the marketplace.

However well equipped with "honest materials" and "intelligent" hands, the studio designer is only partially poised to meet these challenges.

A case can be made for the value of craft in product design only through recognition of this value by collectors and consumers. For the designer, new ways of interacting with producers and consumers will contribute greatly in establishing confidence in investments in high-quality, well-crafted, and innovative products. This will take a close examination of the relevance of craft by the designer.

Notes

1. Conversation with Robert Kuo, September 2006.

2. Jens Bernsen, *Hans J. Wegner* (Dansk Design Center, 1994).

3. Pilar Viladas, "Art in Commerce," *New York Times Style Magazine*, Fall 2006, p. 147.

4. Conversation with Evan Snyderman at R Twentieth Century Design, NY, October 19, 2006.

5. Donald Albrecht, Wendell Castle: *Autoplastic* (R Twentieth Century Design, 2004).

6. Conversation with Wendell Castle at Scottsville Studio, September 12, 2006.

7. James Evans, "Unintentional Iconoclast," (Roger Billcliffe Fine Art, Glasgow Scotland, 1997) from exhibition catalog *Robert Griffith Tables and Sculpture*.

8. Pekka Saarella, *Tapio Wirkkala: Eye, Hand and Thought* (Museum of Arts & Design, Helsinki, Finland, 2001) p. 8.

9. Louise Mitchell, *The Cutting Edge: Fashion from Japan* (Powerhouse Museum, Sydney, Australia, 2005).

10. Helen Rees, "Pattern of Making: Thinking and Making in Industrial Design," *The Culture of Craft* (Manchester University Press, 1997) p. 118–119.

The author gratefully acknowledges the contribution made by Dr. Linda Dugan Partridge.

Inspired by China

Extraordinary craft in the service of artistic vision

text and captions by John Lavine

The high styles of Ming and Qing furniture are the fruit of more than 3000 years of growth and evolution. This furniture is both seductive and intimidating. It is so rich that it seems to offer endless possibilities, and yet its style is so fully realized that a number of artists participating in the "Inspired by China" project chose not to attempt some of its forms. Tom Hucker, for one, shied away from chairs because he didn't feel there was anything more he could say about them; he thought screens offered more opportunity. Likewise, Joe Tracy was intrigued by the Chinese puzzle table but couldn't imagine doing it better than the originals. John Dunnigan spoke for many of the artists when he said, "I want to be careful to not fall into cliché or a superficial treatment."

Nancy Berliner and Ned Cooke, the co-curators of "Inspired by China," envisioned an artists' workshop held in 2005 (see author's note, next page) and the resulting exhibition as important steps in a new cross-cultural exchange between America and China. For the Peabody Essex Museum, the sponsoring institution, this was a very proactive move, stepping beyond their station as a repository and showplace for objects. For the curators, both historians, it was an even more provocative role, acting as true agents of change. As Berliner and Cooke put it: "We trust that this endeavor is only the first of a sustained period of interaction, one that will not homogenize the furniture of the world but highlight regional traditions and inspire new design possibilities."

left: Table with Beam (2005)
Ai Weiwei
Tieli wood, 49.5" x 49.5" x 15.5"
Photo: Ma Xiaochun

Ai Weiwei's *Table with Beam* is an arresting study of tension and balance, with a presence that is both visually striking and visceral. The beam piercing the table is like the surreal evidence of great forces at work, worlds in collision; Michael Hurwitz likened it to the image of a blade of grass driven through a tree, seen in the aftermath of a hurricane. On one level it is the fusion of furniture and architecture, bound together with intricate hidden joinery; viewed another way, both pieces are ancient relics bearing witness to the forceful changes in China. Still, the piece stands inviolate, with a perfect wholeness, the result of extraordinary craftsmanship in the service of a vision.

With this show the seeds have been planted, though it's still too early to know what will take root and mature. It is hardly surprising that the four Chinese artists have been thinking about this furniture for much longer than their sixteen American counterparts, and in general, their work engages the forms and meaning of Ming furniture more confidently than that of the Americans. It's intriguing to imagine what would result from a show premised on a large group of Chinese artists, with a handful of Americans, encountering American Federal furniture.

Within the context of "Inspired by China," there is a certain cohesion to this group of furniture, even if it is widely diverse in style and content. Individually, some pieces are more successful and others underdeveloped, their forms and ideas not fully realized or synthesized. Some fit naturally into the artist's larger body of work, while others seem a curious detour into the exotic. Whether or not these will remain aberrant, or the beginning of a new development in the work, remains to be seen, but its telling that a number of the artists felt compelled to make more than one piece for the exhibition. Garry Bennett made a half dozen, three of which (a table and two chairs) were included in the exhibition, while Michael Cullen, John Dunnigan, Michael Hurwitz, Shao Fan, and Shi Jianmin each made two pieces. Yeung Chan (a Chinese immigrant who has lived and worked in America since the Cultural Revolution) and Michael Puryear each made table-and-chair ensembles. Since the exhibition, Shao Fan and Brian Newell have struck up a friendship and mutual exchange, made easier by their closer proximity (Newell lives in Japan). In a recent telephone conversation, Michael Hurwitz told me he is working on a new series, inspired by the cabinets he made for the show. So may it go. 🐎

John Lavine of Berkeley, CA, is a furniture maker and editor of Woodwork *magazine. He was invited by the curators to attend the 2005 makers' workshop, and from there to follow the progress of the "Inspired by China" exhibition as its official journalist.*

An exhibition catalog, titled Inspired by China *(ISBN 0-87577-205-6), is available through the University of Washington Press (www.washington.edu/uwpress).*

A Long March

Three years in the planning, "Inspired by China: Contemporary Furniture Makers Explore Chinese Traditions" opened at the Peabody Essex Museum (PEM) in Salem, Massachusetts, on October 28, 2006. The show began with a premise similar to the seminal "New American Furniture" exhibition of 1989, in this case bringing together examples of historic Chinese furniture with new works created specifically for the exhibition by artists from the United States, Canada, and China.

There is a long history of cross-cultural influences that have altered and enriched the development of both Chinese and Western furniture. The aesthetics of Chinese design have made an imprint on European and American furniture since the late 17th century, from lacquered surfaces and Chippendale fretwork to the stylized forms of 20th-century Modernism. The sophisticated and refined Chinese furniture that influenced the West was itself the result of a very long evolution involving many foreign influences of form (notably the folding stool and the chair, which had a profoundly transformative effect on a mat-based society) and materials (the availability of hard and dense woods in the 16th century, which made it possible for woodworkers to make the most complex joints in furniture).

However, "Inspired by China" was not conceived in order to showcase contemporary furniture makers whose larger body of work has been inspired by China. Rather, the intention was to create an opportunity for a group of makers to initiate such work. In choosing the

Incense Stand, 17th century
Cloisonne
33.25" x 26.5" x 19"
Photo: Dean Powell

Folding Chair, 18th century
Jumu with boxwood and baitong metal fittings
41" x 22" x 25.5"
Photo: Dean Powell

Altar Table, 17th–18th century
Softwood with incised multicolored lacquer
29.5" x 40.25" x 25.5"
Photo: Dean Powell

Puzzle Tables, seven-piece set, 18th century
Hongmu, burl
31.75" high
Photo: Dean Powell

participants the co-curators, Nancy Berliner (the Peabody Essex Museum curator of Chinese Art) and Edward S. Cooke (Charles F. Montgomery professor of American decorative art and chair of the Department of the History of Art, Yale University), selected artists who they thought would respond to the Chinese collections in a wide range of materials, methods, and conceptual approaches. The American furniture makers, sixteen in number, included seven who had previously appeared in both the "New American Furniture" and the more recent "Maker's Hand" (Museum of Fine Arts, Boston, 2003) exhibitions.

Additionally, participants included one from Canada (Gord Peteran), an American living in Japan (Brian Newell), and four Chinese artists (Ai Weiwei, Tian Jiaqing, Shia Jianmin, and Shao Fan). The Chinese artists all live and work in Beijing; like their American studio furniture counterparts, none of the four trained in traditional apprenticeships, but rather came to furniture making through art schools. One, Tian Jiaqing, began as a scholar of classical Ming furniture.

During a three-day workshop in June 2005, the artists immersed themselves in a wide variety of Chinese furniture at the Peabody and the neighboring Museum of Fine Arts, Boston, as well as a tour of Yin Yu Tang, a 200-year-old Chinese farmhouse reconstructed with all its furnishings on the Peabody grounds. The furniture they examined included not only the better-known Ming and Qing styles, but also wide-ranging examples of vernacular furniture. Additionally, the Peabody invited two Chinese furniture makers from rural Anhui Province (a center of provincial furniture dating back to the Ming dynasty) to give live demonstrations of their craft.

Drum Stool, 17th–18th cent.
Stone
16.25" x 12.75" dia.
Photo: Dean Powell

Screen, 18th century
Wood
68.5" x 46" x 15"
Photo: Dan Gair

Participating in a show such as "Inspired by China" is a high honor, but the recognition comes with a cost. The Peabody brought all of the makers to the museum and covered all their expenses during the three-day workshop. Additionally, it gave them each a modest honorarium for their participation, received upon the delivery of their work. However, each artist invested enormous amounts of time and effort, and all that work was made entirely on speculation. Certainly, there was the expectation that the national exposure of a prestigious exhibition, a handsome catalog, and the possibility of continued exposure as it traveled beyond Boston would provide the cachet to sell the furniture. But all the risk lies with the artists, and as it happened, only two venues beyond the Peabody could be arranged.

After leaving the Peabody Essex Museum, the show will travel to the Museum of Arts & Design in New York City from June 28 through October 28, 2007, then to the Museum of Art in Fort Lauderdale, Florida, where it will run from November 30, 2007 through March 31, 2008. That these are the only other scheduled venues is a disappointment, considering the great investment by all involved to mount the exhibition. Still, the journey of a thousand miles begins with a single footstep, and this is a promising first step.

—*John Lavine*

Roundback Chair, 19th century
Willow, lacquer
22.5" x 19.5" x 10.5", seat height 13.5"
Photo: Dean Powell

Personal Interpretations

*New Scholar's Chairs
and Small Table* (2006)
Yeung Chan
Cherry
Chairs: each 32" x 24" x 21"
Table: 27" x 20" x 18"
Photo: Dean Powell

Yeung Chan has spent many years
studying and making faithful
reproductions of classic Ming chairs
for presentations and teaching
purposes, but for this show he
intentionally avoided that direction,
arriving instead at a contemporary
interpretation more akin to Hans
Wegner (which, in turn, illuminates
how much the development of
Scandinavian modern owed to Chinese
design). While he streamlined the shape of his chairs, Chan took
a traditional approach to their construction, though much of the
work on the classic joints was done using power tools.

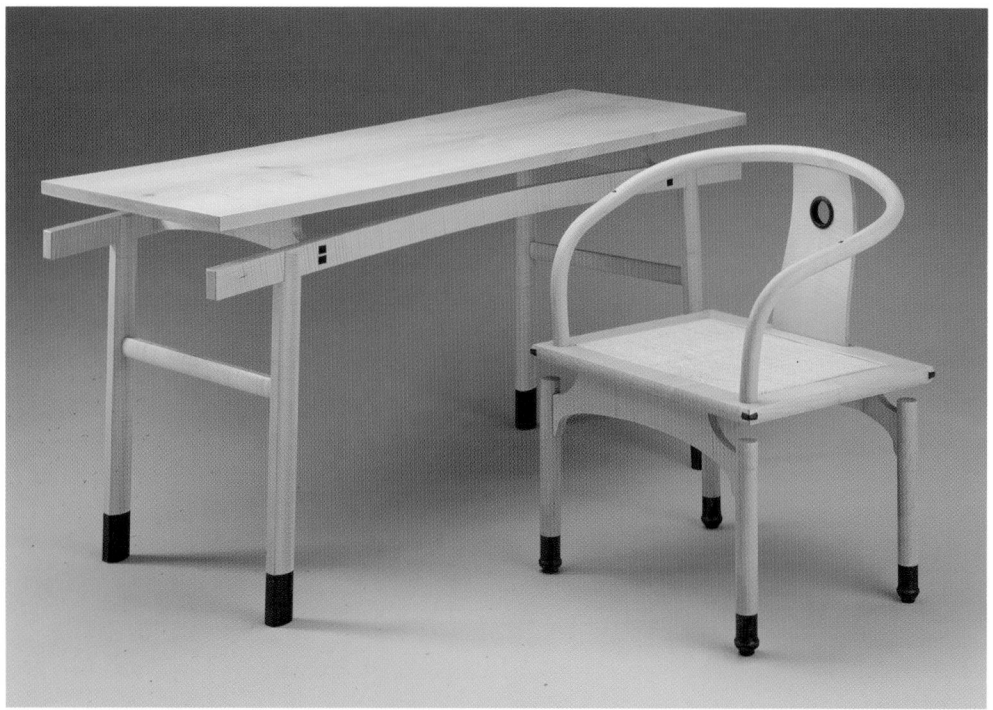

*Wei Jinian Shifu (for
the Master)* (2006)
Michael Puryear
Sycamore, wenge
Chair: 48" x 30" x 24"
Table: 30" x 48" x 24"
Photo: Dean Powell

Though he knew he wanted to make a scholar's desk and chair, Michael Puryear had to
struggle to make his chair his own interpretation rather than an easy synthesis of Ming
design elements. He was ultimately guided by his overarching concepts—a meditation on
the afterlife, and an homage to a passed Tai Chi master/scholar—to give both the desk and
chair a skeletal, almost disembodied quality, an effect that was enhanced by using English
sycamore instead of a traditional dark wood, and by creating lifts in the understructures to
elevate the seat and the desktop.

(left) *Silk Route Stool* (2006)
John Dunnigan
White oak, brass, leather
15" x 37" x 11"
Photo: Mark Johnston

(below) *Standing Desk* (2005)
John Dunnigan
Padauk, brass
48" x 66" x 20"
Photo: Dean Powell

John Dunnigan is another longtime student of furniture history. His first attraction was to the folding stool, not only as an object in itself but because of its historical and cultural significance. However, he also has a long interest in writing desks, and ultimately this larger, more formal piece became the focus of his attention. His *Standing Desk* nicely balances several Chinese elements—the traditional pair of cabinets embellished with oversized hardware—with shaped stands and an elevated writing surface that are identifiably Dunnigan's. Only after he had delivered this work to the museum, and very close to deadline, did he return to the stool. He built *Silk Route Stool* very quickly, using just the appropriate level of craftsmanship, and thereby captured a real vitality that is often lost in larger, more labored work.

The Allure of Technique

Cicada Cabinet (2006)
Brian Newell
Zitan
37.5" x 42" x 12"
Photo: Dennis Helmar

Brian Newell's work is known, as curator Ned Cooke aptly puts it, "for its obsessive attention to craftsmanship in service to personal, almost mysterious cabinets that seem animated." His *Cicada Cabinet* is no exception. Inspired by a curved pendant given to Newell by the Chinese maker Shao Fan after a visit to Beijing, the cabinet stands on eight shaped legs, the top section stretched wing-like over a lower upturned lattice shelf of a traditional Chinese pattern. Every inch of surface is curved, carved, or incised. Indeed, all the details crowding the diminutive form can be disconcerting, like peering at an insect under a lens.

(left) Chair for a Small Important Person (2005)
Garry Knox Bennett
Rosewood, gold-plated copper and brass,
nautilus shell, epoxy, paint
28.5" x 22.5" x 19"
Photo: Dean Powell

(below) Altar Table (2005)
Garry Knox Bennett
Honduran rosewood, California walnut, bamboo,
aluminum, copper, paint
40" x 96" x 16"
Photo: Dean Powell

Of traditional joinery, Garry Knox Bennett says,
"I can understand why people do that stuff, but if
I'm doing that then I'm not thinking about anything
else but joinery, and I don't have time for that." *Chair
for a Small Important Person* required considerable
attention to the method of joining parts together,
but Bennett in typical fashion shunned traditional
joinery, employing epoxy and metal fasteners instead.
Likewise, his *Altar Table* is carefully engineered for
structural integrity. For example, the ends of the
timber bamboo legs that are joined to the painted
aluminum brackets are carefully reinforced with
wooden plugs epoxied in place, then slotted and
attached with ornamented bolts that thread from
both sides of the bamboo into tapped holes in the
aluminum—a completely modern solution using
non-traditional materials and methods.

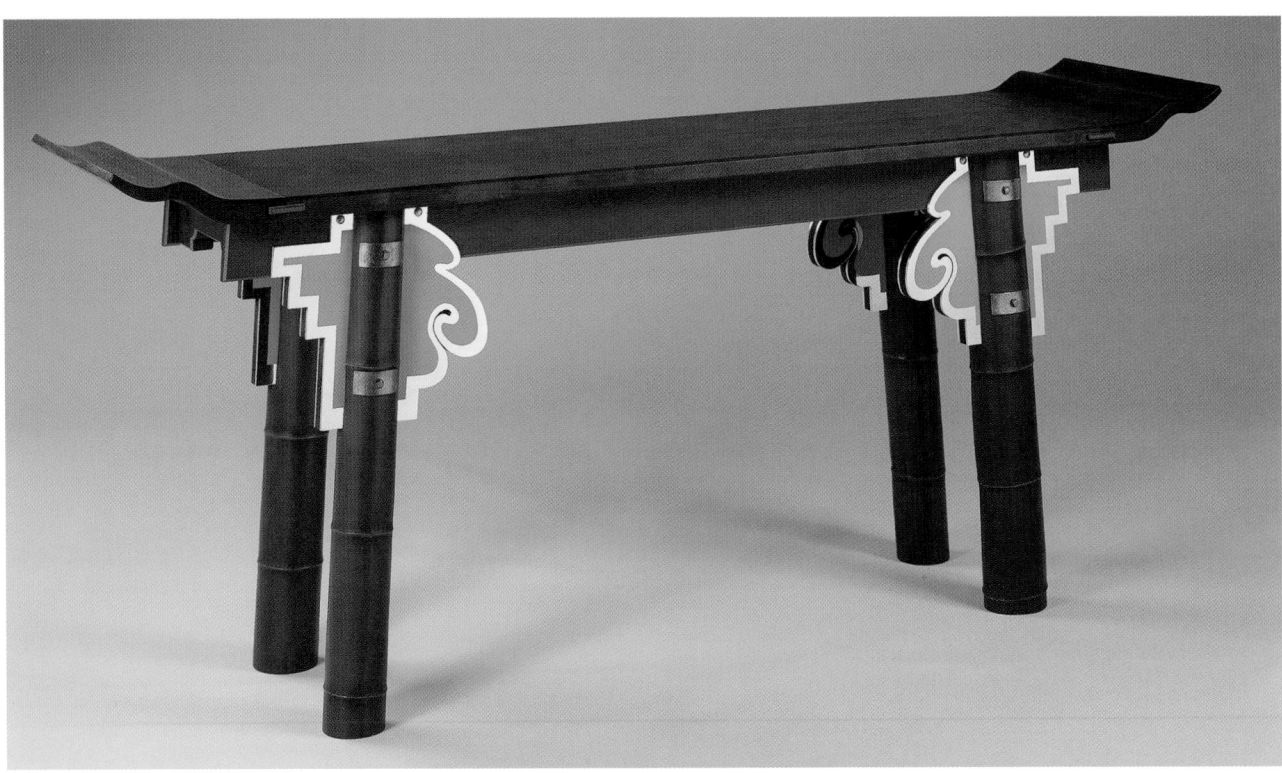

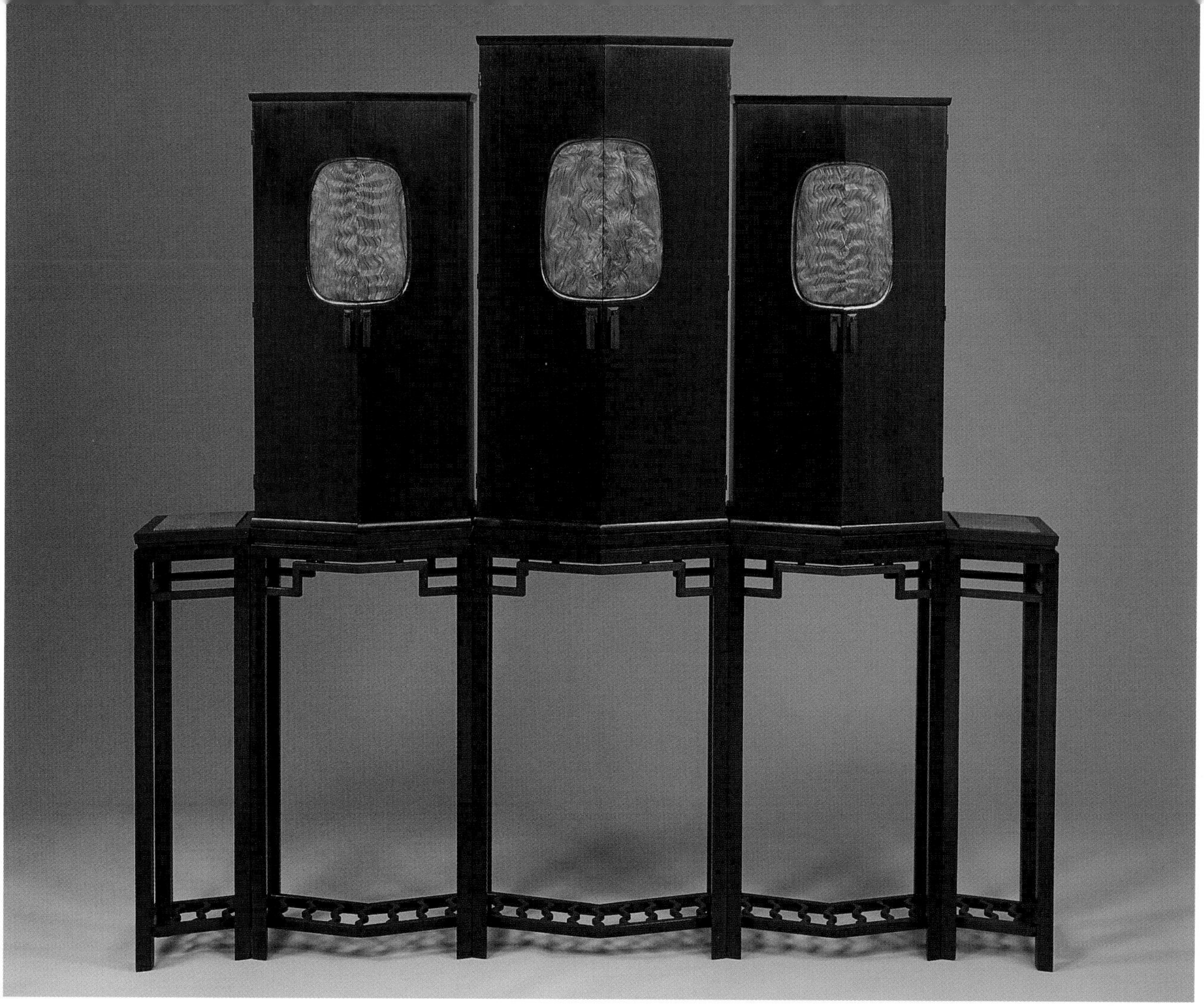

Three Case Studies (2006)
Joe Tracy
Wenge, split sequoia redwood, Indonesian red palm,
Lebanon cedar, walnut, Damascus steel, silver leaf
72" x 20" x 16"
Photo: Dean Powell

Joe Tracy's cabinet pays elaborate attention to materials and surfaces, both inside and out. The cabinet (actually, an ensemble of seven pieces inspired by both the puzzle table and folding screens) is reminiscent of English Arts and Crafts cases, but is replete with Chinese motifs (cracked ice, cloud lifts, and so on), as well as with complicated joints. As Tracy explains: "I've done other pieces that had that amount of detail in them, but not too often. I put 1,100 hours into this piece, which is kind of stunning, and a lot of the hours take place in an area that you don't even really look at. It's a Chinese-style joint that I modified that connects the legs to the stretchers... the joints weren't easy to cut and to get them to fit right. But I felt it was important to be faithful to the look and the structure of that joint."

Tracy also was influenced by his previous work with curly redwood: there was a quality in the material that he wanted to capture and feature. To do this he used a froe, but unlike a green-wood chair maker, who splits straight-grained material, Tracy's goal was to unleash the energy in the most unruly redwood he could find, working as he put it "on the cusp of failure." Juxtaposed with his intricate joints, this workmanship of risk makes it clear that craftsmanship and technical precision, though often used synonymously, are not the same.

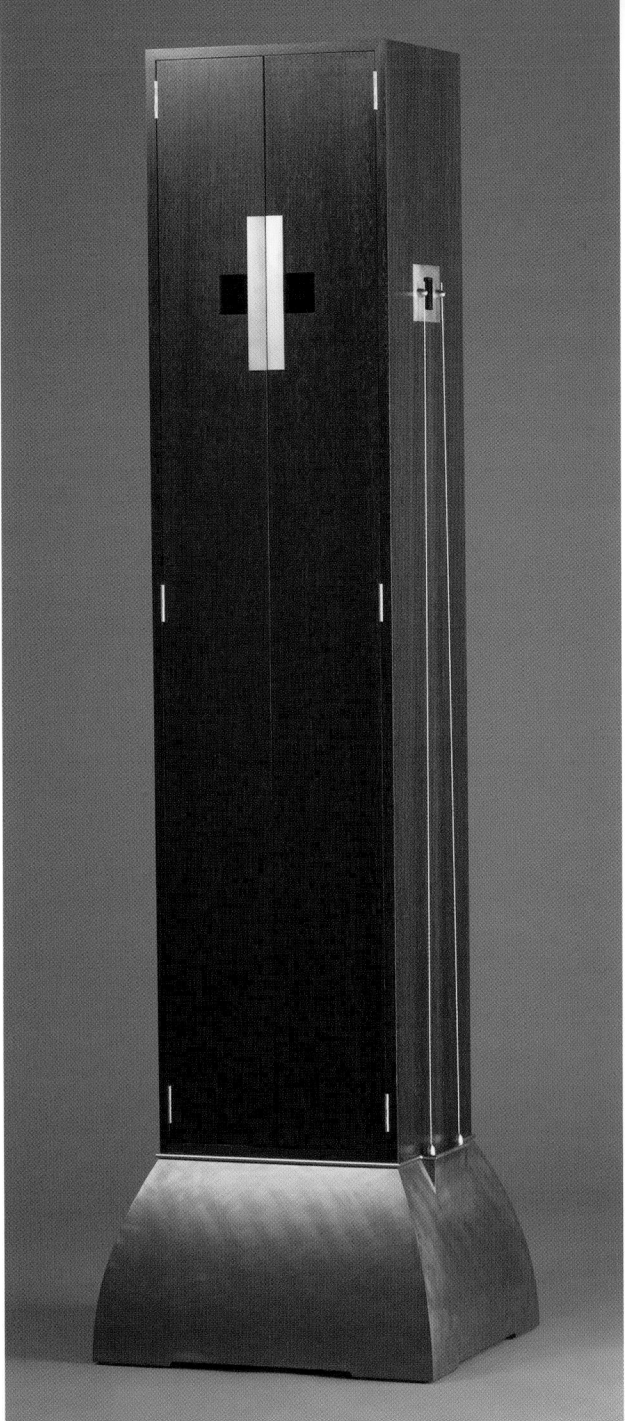

Material Concerns

The Chinese Piece (2006)
Michael Hurwitz
Bamboo, zelkova, elm, Damascus iron, bronze
78" x 36" x 24"
Photo: Dean Powell

Michael Hurwitz envisioned two tall cabinets for the exhibition, in keeping with the traditional Chinese pairing in a household. He was fascinated by the translucent quality of the cracked ice motif so prevalent in Ming furniture, and this became the starting point for a composition exploring varying degrees of density: a solid, heavily figured zelkova panel below an open cracked-ice grillwork and opposite a woven lattice. Every choice he made for that first cabinet left many other possibilities set aside, and a number of these were incorporated into the second cabinet (not shown), completed too late for the catalog but just in time for the opening of the show.

Untitled (2006)
Richard Prisco
Wenge, bamboo, nickel-plated steel,
stainless steel, graphite
72" x 14" x 12"
Photo: Joseph Byrd

Richard Prisco uses a mix of materials to good effect, both in the visual contrast of steel with the wenge carcase of his cabinet and in the conceptual contrast with its suggested function. He was intrigued by the portability of a Chinese apothecary chest, but his cabinet stand, intractable and monolithic, is rooted to a heavy steel base and defies the carrying bar that is meant to move the piece.

Reclining Dragon (2005)
Tian Jiaqing
Huanghuali
33" x 34" x 174"
Photo: Yi Yan Nanjin

Reclining Dragon, Tian Jiaqing's massive altar table, honors Ming furniture and a special piece of huanghuali, a 4-inch thick, 33-inch wide, and 15-foot long plank cut from a log that came to the artist, as he puts it, "after a real saga." According to Tian, who was for many years a scholar of Ming furniture before he began to make it, "The proportions of a true Ming-style piece of furniture are exact and artistic. It's actually a deceptively simple style, but the proportions are really very exacting, it's about a harmony of shape… In typical Ming style, the joinery itself became an artwork within an artwork. Also, the wood itself has personality and life. The joinery pieces were seen as part of a family. So much so that matching the two sides of a joint was called 'renjia,' or 'recognizing home.'"

Between Nature and Artifice

(right) Star Table (2005)
Michael Cullen
Red eucalyptus
18" x variable width
Photo: Dennis Helmar

After experiencing the Chinese furniture at the Peabody Essex, Michael Cullen resolved that he would make a piece that "left the tree in the wood." He worked with a sawyer in northern California to cut a thick, star-shaped cross-section from a giant eucalyptus tree. The process of completing his *Star Table* was a balancing act between nature and artifice, requiring considerable restraint: removing signs of human intervention (from the felling and slicing of the tree)

and cleaning up loose fibers in all the cavities of the stump that the eye would find distracting, all done with a light touch so as not to look worked but in reality requiring a great amount of work. As in several other pieces, the craftsmanship involved lies in altering the surfaces just enough to maintain the illusion of the natural, while actually removing the natural.

Cullen's second piece, inspired by the Chinese puzzle tables and the cracked ice motif, contrasts a freely carved surface of irregular shapes with the exact, angular milk-painted planes of the tables' bases. While the various configurations of the tables always have a continuous top surface, each variation creates a different pattern of spaces between the bases.

(left) Quintet with Cracked Ice (2006)
Michael Cullen
Mahogany, paint
20" x 38" x 38"
Photo: Dennis Helmar

Dragon Stool (2006)
Judy McKie
Indiana limestone
19" x 20.5" x 20.5"
Photo: Dean Powell

The only artist to actually work in stone was Judy McKie. Although she was impressed by the complexity and intricacy of Chinese joints, she also responded to the simple rounded form of a stone drum stool, and this became the perfect vehicle for her relief-carved animal motif, a stylized dragon that is quintessential McKie yet very much at home alongside the Ming stools.

Stool (2005)
Shi Jianmin
Stainless steel
20.5" x 59" x 55"
Photo: Ma Xiaochun

Stool by Shi Jianmin takes a different approach to the contradictions of the original Chinese furniture. It relates to the traditional Chinese art of collecting and critiquing stones for such things as their qualities of aliveness; made of stainless steel, it sits transformed from the organic into something curiously otherworldly, like a meteorite. But he is also aware of the artifice; as he says, "In art-design I feel that the primary visual effect is definitely to create a sense of the piece being a work of art. The first reaction should be 'Ah, this is art,' and only then 'Ah, this also can be used...'" Shi Jianmin's stainless steel chair is an even more extreme movement away from the aesthetics and dictates of wood. He designed it from a pen-and-ink sketch that tried to capture "the inner life of the stone" in the flow of the metal.

Chair (2005)
Shi Jianmin
Stainless steel
84" x 36" x 36"
Photo: Ma Xiaochun

Screen #1 (2006)
Tom Hucker
Swiss pearwood, English yew, bronze
69" x 111" x 1.5"
Photo: Dean Powell

The tension between nature and artifice is implicit in Chinese furniture, but that tension was made explicit in Tom Hucker's screen. The surround for the screen is Swiss pearwood, worked to a fine finish and joined to make the frames, which contain large panels of English yew, rough-sawn and sandblasted to emphasize their grain. The open lattice of branches seems to grow out of the frame, like young shoots on a fallen log. However, these branches are intermixed with bronze castings of other branches and lengths of bronze rod, making a superstructure that is at once natural and highly artificial. If you look closely at some of the castings, you will see

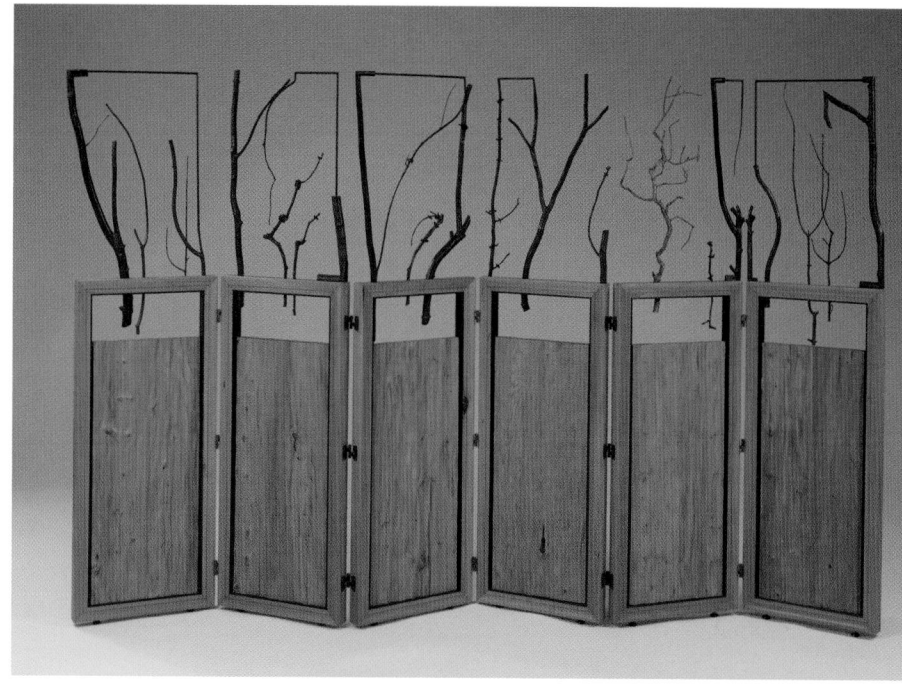

flashings—evidence of a broken mold during the casting process—but these were left in place as a matter of what Hucker called "honesty to process," while the green-patinated bronze branch was actually fabricated from seven different castings that were welded together and meticulously ground to remove all evidence of the fabrication process. Layers of craft and non-craft, artifice and nature, play off against each other.

Cracked-Ice Puzzle Tables (2005)
Silas Kopf
White Oak, East Indian rosewood, various veneers
Six pieces, each 34" high
Photo: Dean Powell

Silas Kopf's *Cracked-Ice Puzzle Table* plays the tangram shapes of the individual pieces against the geometry of his marquetry pattern. The artifice of surfaces is at the heart of Kopf's work, which is cleverly conceived to read as though the surface of each table was shattered at a specific point, from which ever-increasing pieces of ice expand outward. To complete the thought, a trompe-l'oeil piece of parchment on one of the tables says, in Chinese calligraphy, "The artfulness of the cracked-ice tables shatters to pieces the uncarved block."

Cultural Cross-Purposes

Vanity (2006)
Wendy Maruyama
Pau ferro, mixed media, video
42" x 16" x 16"
Photo: Dean Powell

Wendy Maruyama's *Vanity* also considers the artifice of surface and image, but in this case from a cultural and gendered point of view. Her cabinet is both a make-up stand and a stand-in for a small Asian woman (complete with a cleverly distorted version of traditional horse-hoof feet that read as bound feet). The framework at top holds a two-way mirror backed by a small LCD screen on which plays a video of an Asian woman (Maruyama's sister) applying eye make-up, alternately transforming herself into a more Western or a more Oriental look. Because the mirror is two-way, the viewer simultaneously sees a reflection of his/her own face.

Sea and Sky Altar Coffer (2006)
Bonnie Bishoff and J. M. Syron
Mahogany, polymer clay
26" x 32" x 18"
Photo: Dean Powell

Like Tian Jiaqing, a number of artists were drawn to the altar table for inspiration. Both Garry Bennett and the team of Bonnie Bishoff and J. M. Syron evoke a similar fanciful feeling by their choice of materials and design: bright colors, stylized forms, non-traditional materials such as polymer clay and painted aluminum. Formally, both reference the everted flanges of a traditional altar table, an element that Bennett has incorporated into his tables for many years. Additionally, the casework that Syron made for their piece references the leg ornamentation of a quirky regional piece of 16th–17th century furniture—an example of the way in which some artists gravitated to the less formal and less overpowering Ming forms.

Alter Altar Table (2006)
Clifton Monteith
Oak, willow twigs, urushi lacquer
35" x 36" x 22"
Photo: Dennis Helmar

Clifton Monteith was attracted to a worn-out piece of country furniture, albeit one that still had an important ritualistic use. For Monteith, the choice was very personal: "Not too long ago I lost both of my parents and my wife's parents, all in the course of three years… The Chinese family altar is an institutionalized way of bringing that question up, not just through a period of grief, but through a continual remembrance." He further explains: "But there was another reason: because it was in bad condition, and I love things that have deteriorated… and so I thought, 'This is perfect!' A family altar table made out of really pedestrian materials in a very elegant way—at least from my point of view." This is a perfect expression of the two Asian concepts of "wabi" and "sabi," typically merged in the West as "wabi-sabi," an appreciation of transient beauty in the physical world, manifest in the modest, imperfect, or even decayed, reflecting the irreversible flow of life in the spiritual world. And, as Monteith notes, "My materials are very pedestrian. The lacquer, which many people think of as a very high-class surface, is really just sap from a poison sumac tree. And my willow trees are just collected from the ditch next to the road." The success of the piece derives from this union of concept and materials.

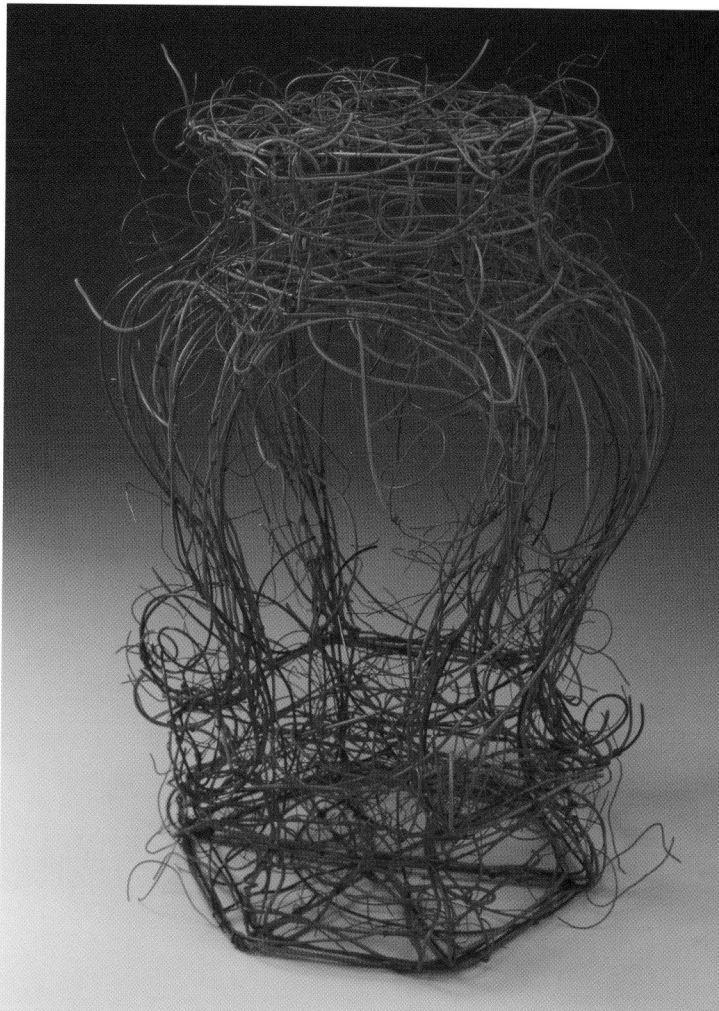

Inception (2006)
Gord Peteran
Electrical wire
31" x 24" x 24"
Photo: Dean Powell

The gestural quality in Monteith's work with willow has an unlikely counterpart in the incense stand made by Gord Peteran, who has tried to incorporate the freedom of sketching in his recent work. And there are other interesting correspondences. Monteith uses red symbolically in the lacquered section of his table, and speaks of looking down "into the heart of the matter" through the open grid in the altar top. Peteran's red electrical-wire construction invites a similar looking below the surface to "the complicated arteries of the fragile China we might not see." But what he finds there is not the wabi-sabi of ancient artifacts; it is the post-war glut of "made in China" consumables and the equally unrelenting push of hi-tech "progress" that isravaging China's environment even as it promises Western-style prosperity.

Curiously Red... (2006)
Hank Gilpin
Elm, color, magnets
36" x 76" x 18"
Photo: Dean Powell

Hank Gilpin saw red in a personal way when contemplating this piece. He already had a thin, distorted plank of elm salvaged from a very large tree that had been a casualty of development, and this became the centerpiece for his meditation on the loss of life... of trees and people. He constructed a table to support the elm board with extended rails that evoke a stretcher bearing the plank-top victim; the whole is suffused in red stain that drips blood-like down the legs. To secure the top to the base without piercing the top's fragile surface, Gilpin inset magnets in both, using a non-traditional (but non-intrusive) technology in the service of his idea.

U-Shaped Altar Table (2005)
Shao Fan
Elm
36.5" x 69.625" x 45"
Photo: Ma Xiaochun

For Shao Fan, the altar table has a layered meaning and his response is nuanced. In a 1996 show in China called "Chair(?)," Shao Fan deconstructed the classic Ming chair, which he felt embodied the essence of Chinese philosophy, and recombined it with contemporary materials and design to express the cultural changes facing his country. Paradoxically, both respect for traditional methods and a questioning of traditional values coexist in the work. In *U-Shaped Altar Table* he pointedly subverts the traditional place and function of the altar, while at the same time his meticulous work honors the tradition of craftsmanship. His other contribution to the show, *Round Stool* (not shown), is a more direct homage to change, and the role of craft becomes one of facilitating the transformation rather than being in uneasy tension with the intent of the object.

Porch lighting by Dan Radven,
p. 90

Bespoke Interiors

The good commission adds an extra dimension

interviews by Oscar Fitzgerald

The publicly visible output of the studio furniture maker is the gallery piece—work done on speculation, for exhibition, for publication, and for promotion. This is important work since it is where makers develop and display new ideas, unfettered by the limitations of the client commission, and for most makers it also represents a serious and somewhat risky investment. The maker might, and often does, end up living with the piece in his own home.

Speculative work, however, eliminates two crucial elements in the furniture-making equation: there is no client, and there is no fee. The other kind of work, which has been commissioned and presumably paid for, has always been the bread-and-butter of the working maker. In the 17th century it was called "bespoke," meaning it was spoken for in advance of being made. The client adds a critical dimension to this kind of work, not only by way of the space where the work is meant to fit, but also by way of the collaboration with the artist that animates good commissions. While makers may yearn for the client who offers a completely free hand, that is almost never the case. And the truth is, the work is most often made better by the necessity to pay attention to what the client says he needs and wants, how much he wants to pay, and when he needs it done. The best commissions become collaborations in the highest sense of the word, with each party supplying critical elements the other cannot provide for himself, and the result being greater than either could accomplish alone.

A steady diet of speculative work is limiting in another way: with the exception of the one-man show, and the career retrospective, one rarely sees more than one piece of furniture from each maker. This does not convey the range of work the maker is capable of doing, nor does it show the harmony that can result when a single intelligence designs and makes everything in the interior.

With all of that in mind, the editors of Furniture Studio issued an open call during autumn 2006 for makers to submit images of bespoke interiors they had completed. We received a wide range of responses, a few of which are shown on the following pages. We had anticipated that we would be seeing commissions, but we had not anticipated the surprise of artists' own homes—furnished with a combination of unsold pieces, spouse-commissioned work, and experimental work. This too met our definition, interiors that spring from a single creative mind, and you will see several artist homes on these pages as well.

—*John Kelsey, editor*

Artist: Arnt Arntzen
Vancouver, British Columbia, Canada
Client: Valerie Arntzen

Artist's own home, ongoing since 1994

In 1994 Arnt Arntzen and three fellow artists bought an old bakery to turn it into studio space downstairs and four apartments upstairs. Except for the dining chairs, Arntzen built all the furniture in his apartment, including the lighting. He likes to show off his living quarters so clients can see examples of his designs. His scrap-yard finds keep materials costs down while adding character and patina to his work. Copper mesh shades the lights on the chandelier and the tiki torches on the bar.

Perforated metal forms the back of a chair and the front of the bar, while parts of helicopter wings support the maple bar top. A bent airplane propeller holds up the side table. Tiller disks become the bases for bar stools, and embedded glass balls from an abandoned mirror factory punctuate the steel shade on the table lamp. Sheathing cut from a roll of scrap copper covers the base of Arntzen's signature rocket table. The kitchen sink is an industrial castoff, and the TV is mounted to the adjustable arm of an X-ray machine.

Arntzen also uses salvaged wood, mostly from blown-down trees that he cuts himself, but also from buildings. He shaped the top of his side table from a piece of wood cut from a 20-foot beam of dark red, South American ekki. The bar stool seats are alder and the chair bottom is maple. He picked up ebony scraps from a guitar factory to make handles for his maple kitchen cabinets.

An exception to scavenging was the black walnut that Arntzen bought from an East Coast distributor for the prototype dining table. He liked the irregular edges of the boards, and rather than waste good wood sawing the slabs to fit together, he shaped a steel strip to match the waney edges, leaving a gap to allow for wood movement. The tabletop rests on cut-down streetlamp posts fitted with oak feet.

Ball bearings appear everywhere in Arntzen's work: as feet on his TV cabinet, tables, lamps, and seating; as finials on the crest rail of his chairs, and as the nose of the rocket supporting his table.

A giant roller bearing from a huge electric motor makes the base of his table lamp. Playing marbles as a child, he always lusted after the precious steelies, but you had to hit the other guy's marble at least ten times to get one. He never did, but now as an adult he uses them whenever he can.

When artists make their own furniture it often ends up sold. Arntzen's wife, Valerie, did not want to lose the rocket table so he signed it and gave it to her for her birthday. He also built a cherry and rosewood chest for her while helping Peter Pierobon during a dovetail workshop at Haystack Mountain School of Crafts in Maine. A labor of love, he exposed the dovetails for the case and hand-cut dovetails for all the drawers. These two pieces won't leave for sure, and as the other furniture in the house acquires the patina of age, the chance of anything else slipping out the door declines as well.

Artist: Stephen Hogbin
Wiarton, Ontario, Canada

Private Residence 2001–2004
Collingwood, Ontario, Canada

Stephen Hogbin's accountant recommended him to the client who had just built a 9,500-square-foot house. After a walk-through with the owner, it was clear that doing the whole house was too big a job so they decided to begin with the 1,000-square-foot entertainment room. Elements in the countryside where the house was located inspired Hogbin's design. The wavy façade of the cabinet doors on the wall above the bar and kitchen area suggests the sun rising over an undulating ski slope. The blue cabinets below evoke ice. He cut the cabinet facades with a specially designed milling machine, freehand in the manner of an abstract expressionist sculpture.

The driveway up to the house passes through an apple orchard and the staircase, narrow at the bottom and flaring out at the top, recalls a wooden apple basket. It was Hogbin's first spiral staircase. His signature turnings form the newel post; the center post that holds the steps terminates in a point, like a ship's prow that acknowledges a once-major industry in the area. Hogbin designed the complete interior and built the specialized cabinetry and staircase himself, but left the routine work, such as the stone floor and bar façade, to other craftsmen.

Midway through the project the clients asked Hogbin to work on several special jobs elsewhere in the house, including two more staircases, a banquet table and chairs, a china cabinet, and side tables in the main entrance hall. The most challenging request was for a fireplace surround—challenging because what Hogbin had in mind was different from what the clients wanted. After going back and forth several times and looking at images in magazines, they arrived on the same page. The lighted, arrow-shaped niches on either side of the fireplace are formed by turnings cut into quarters. Although the clients joke that it is their design, in the end it was a collaboration, a true symbiosis. Hogbin says he never had to compromise his design sense at any time during the process.

Having done many public commissions in the 1980s and 1990s where he was constantly having to satisfy endless and often mindless committees, Hogbin finds working with private clients much easier at this stage in his life. He observes that while bureaucracies require detailed plans, a quick sketch or a rough model is enough for the client who has come to trust the artist's judgment.

Artist: Douglas W. Jones
Los Lunas, NM
Client: Dee Dee O'Brien and
Dennis Sanders

Stair landing alcove, 2004, Shelburne, VT

While teaching at the Shelburne Art Center, Doug Jones was approached by one of his students, Dee Dee O'Brien, to design furniture for a unique space in her home. At the top of a staircase an 80-foot-wide circular alcove looked out on a spectacular view of Lake Champlain. During the renovation of the 1920s cottage, an architect had designed built-in seating with bookshelves below, but the clients wanted something more decorative. Wrestling with countless curved shapes, Jones came up with two models for seating. He was delighted when the clients picked the elliptical shape that was his favorite. He chose a curve that would relate to the bay but with enough contrast to make the benches stand out from the wall. The chamfered edges of the slats under the sloping crest rails echoed the beadboard on the walls. Jones adjusted the widths of the slats so as not to end up with an undersized slat at the end of the sloping crest rail. The slats were attached to a bendable plywood core.

While the two curved benches echo the surrounding architecture, they are also replete with subtle, riparian references. Their elliptical shape evokes waves or sails, and the spiral carving on the hand rests suggests nautilus shells. Jones chose to piece the crest rails rather than use bent laminations because the piecing technique reminded him of similarly constructed ship railings. Moreover, he liked the variation in the wood grain and the way the light reflected off the different sections. The sloping crest rails on the benches also recalled Victorian fainting couches, which imparted a formal and decorative appearance clearly visible from the first-floor entrance.

The clients visited Jones's shop several times during construction and were delighted with the progress of the work. They did pick out the upholstery fabric and specified unpainted mahogany, but other than that they gave him free rein.

A pedestal table completed the space. The clients had envisioned one big enough to play games on, but in order not to detract from the benches all agreed on a smaller pedestal that Jones had used with variations for other clients. He painted the pedestal to pick up on the existing wall color and make it stand out from the benches. To add interest, he carved stripes on the shaft and concentric circles on the base, an unconscious reference to ripples in the lake.

Artist: Craig Thibodeau
San Diego, CA

Living room cabinets, 2006, San Diego, CA

Craig Thibodeau's realtor referred these clients to him. They viewed the work on his website but mostly trusted the realtor's recommendation. They had just bought a condominium and wanted to use space under the stairs for much-needed storage. They had very specific needs including a shoe rack, filing cabinets, and space for china, books, and art. Other than that, they gave Thibodeau a free hand—the ideal clients. He prepared a three-dimensional, computer-generated design, which they immediately liked with only a few minor modifications. They did not want a tunnel effect as they walked into the living room adjacent to the cabinet, so he stepped it back from a four-foot depth under the steps to about two feet at the end. He included seats in the niches designed for wall-hung art, and added a mini-office and computer area at one end of the unit. Four separate dimmer switches control lights over the display shelves. He gave the clients a choice of woods, and they picked African pomele sapele, and cherry. The black-lacquered base molding and cornice strip outline the piece and set it off from the rest of the room. During the project the clients periodically visited Thibodeau's shop to follow the progress, but they never demanded any changes.

An engineer turned furniture maker, Thibodeau has focused primarily on commissions but accepts some high-end, built-in work as a nice break from his marquetry-embellished furniture. This cabinet took four and a half months to complete in his one-man shop, even though he contracted out all the finishing. The 33-foot-long unit breaks down into 15 separate sections, small enough to fit into the elevator that serves the 6th-floor apartment. The commission also included some cabinet work in the kitchen in a compatible style.

Artist: Loy Martin
Palo Alto, CA
Client: Roman Weil

Dining Room, 2005, Chicago, IL

Roman Weil was building a 400-square-foot second home near San Francisco, when his architect asked Loy Martin to make a table and six chairs that would fold up and hang on the wall. Weil obviously liked the results because seven years later, when he was getting married and moving into a new house in Chicago, he called Martin to do another dining room set, this time in a bigger space.

Martin proposed a design inspired by an early 19th century Federal pedestal table that could be expanded with three leaves to a racetrack shape, in order to fit the irregular octagonal room. The diamond motif in the center of the table, repeated on the backs of the chairs, picked up the diamond pattern of the leaded glass windows in the house. Martin veneered the table with quilted mahogany radiating from a central medallion.

The book-matched mahogany on the front and back of the bent-laminated chair splats complemented the rich mahogany tabletop. Ten chairs fit comfortably around the fully extended table, but the client wanted two extras that he could use on opposite sides of his nearby partner's desk

Two-thirds of the way through the project the client suddenly sold his house and moved into a lavish new condominium, but he still wanted to complete the commission. Since the original space had no room for a proper sideboard, Martin had proposed a tall china cabinet and two console tables. The new condominium, however, could accommodate a sideboard so the cabinet was cancelled. Martin combined quilted mahogany left over from the dining table with rosewood to blend nicely with the other furniture. He fitted the sideboard with compartments to store the client's silver.

Weil decided to go ahead with the original plan for a pair of Macassar ebony console tables with pear wood inlay, but without drawers. Even though he had no room in the new dining room for both

tables, Weil had children and grandchildren who would eventually inherit the furniture. One daughter in particular had her eye on the console tables.

After everything was installed, the daughter suggested that a mirror should hang over the sideboard. Although he initially thought that a mirror was too much with all of the glass in the room, Martin remembered an antique mirror with cloudy glass in his own collection and decided that it might work. He collaborated on the mirror with Frances Binnington, a specialist in verre eglomise then working in California. Since Weil was a lifelong wine enthusiast, Martin selected the image of grape stomping from the September pages of a Medieval book of hours. Binnington treated the mirror for a romantic, smoky reflection that softened the whole effect.

The last Martin heard, Weil was retiring, selling his condominium, and building yet another house in California.

Artist: Dan Radven
Hamilton, MT

Porch lighting, outside seating, and living room accents, 2006, Hamilton, MT

The clients had seen Dan Radven's metalwork in a local gallery, and commissioned him to make a fireplace screen for a house they were renovating. Picking up on the exposed dovetail joinery in the house, Radven designed an iron frame with dovetails at each corner. Influenced by the Arts and Crafts movement, the joinery was the ornament. Sympathetic to the natural wood in the house, he recycled the iron from a 19th century wagon-wheel tire, softened and abraded from its original use. He fashioned the door handles out of stacked leather disks, an idea from an antique carving mallet.

Pleased with the results, the clients next wanted a table with a free edge, like the work of George Nakashima. Since walnut does not grow in Montana, Radven found a California source that

Elin Christopherson, a glass blower in Oakland, California, supplied the green glass. A patio in the back provided a similar transition from the nearby creek to the house. Radven designed cantilevered brackets holding cedar benches to echo both the meandering stream and the timbered house construction.

One last project: the bar was already built, but it needed stools. Starting with a speculative stool the clients saw in his studio, Radven sent off sketches, and after adjusting the seat configuration, made a mockup for approval. The keyhole shape is a recurring signature in his work. He could have welded the stools together but prefers the way exposed joints highlight each element. As a metalsmith, Radven called upon a local furniture maker to reproduce his prototype seat in reclaimed pine.

It was a nice project because it provided a chance for growth. Rather than a single commission, which is Radven's standard fare, he designed a number of unique pieces in response to particular spaces. He succeeded because he established a good working relationship with the clients early on, and they trusted his decisions—important since they were in residence only occasionally while the work went on.

had a perfect slab of claro walnut requiring very little trimming. The clients chose a base he had adapted from an earlier console table, where the shelf under the walnut slab serves as a stretcher that penetrates each of the three curved legs with a keyed through tenon. Using reclaimed steel, Radven folded and upset the edges for greater strength and a more substantial appearance.

The four hanging porch lanterns suggest tree branches and serve as a transition from the forested site into the wood-timbered home.

Artist: Paul Sasso
Almo, KY
Client: Sandy Sasso

Artist's home, 1984 and ongoing

When Paul Sasso took some time off from art school in Canada to work as carpenter, he developed a passion for building. He loves wood and the instant gratification gained from working this medium. He began building his house in 1984 and now, 20-plus years later, he is almost finished. He characterizes it as a tiny toy like a Lego house. It has lots of built-ins, particularly shelves for books and decorative objects. It is filled with interesting details, many of them classically inspired. The windows are framed with classical quarter columns and the doorways are flanked by fluted pilasters. The walls are embellished with wainscot panels and abundant base and crown moldings.

When Sandy Sasso says that the house is the perfect backdrop for Paul's flamboyant furniture, it is at first hard to believe. But after a closer look, the connection is clear. Sasso has lavished the same attention to detail on his house as he has on his furniture, and has imbued both with multiple layers of meaning. Like his classically inspired

woodwork, *Greco-Roman Happy Meal* starts with a classical title and a classical vase but out of it comes a bright zinnia copied from a 17th century French engraving. Fire is a common motif in Sasso's work, not as a destructive force, but rather as a symbol of excitement and passion. The carved wooden fabrics, his signature motif, evolved from a study of 15th and 16th century German carving. The cloth carved on the Greco-Roman pedestal is covered with symbols from Catholic vestments— Sasso was once a Catholic.

The fire image on the candelabra, aptly named *Fuel*, is one of the few instances where Sasso uses the idea to connote destruction. When one of the huge oaks that inhabit his part of Kentucky dies, tree men cut off the limbs and haul away the wood to be burned as fuel. This piece pays homage to those majestic, 300-year-old trees and to their afterlife.

All of Sasso's furniture is left over from shows and waits to be sold—except the coffee table. Although Sandy ordered the table many years ago, it arrived only recently as a Christmas present. Sasso likes the tripod table form, and several similar tables are scattered around the house. On this table the third legs join like a cell in the process of dividing. Some people are reminded of Michelangelo's *Creation of Adam* in the Sistine Chapel, not what Sasso imagined but the sort of connection he hopes people will make. Are those red crosses on the coffee table legs, or are they Band-Aids?

Sandy Sasso finds her husband's furniture warm, human in scale, and easy to live with. She enjoys moving it around to view in different lights and different backdrops. *Happy Meal* sometimes ends up in the bathroom. They are like people, she says—complex, interesting, and full of fire.

Artist: James Schriber
New Milford, CT
Client: Arlene and Harvey Caplan

Bathroom, 2006, Morristown, NJ

Arlene and Harvey Caplan had purposely left much of the interior of their new home, designed by Hugh Newell Jacobsen, a modernist architect, unfinished so that they could hire studio artists to fill the empty rooms. They commissioned a dining room set from Wendell Castle, a nursery from Tommy Simpson, a bedroom from Ed Zucca, a guest room from Peter Pierobon, and a bathroom from Thomas Hucker.

Active in the Museum of Arts & Design in New York, Arlene had been impressed by the lobby desk James Schriber had built for it. She had asked him to work on several of their earlier houses, and he had built some cabinets for other bathrooms in this house, so it was not surprising that she commissioned him to do a complete interior… of a bathroom. Schriber found this project a little out of his line, but he had a long history with the clients and so he looked at it as a way to stretch his capabilities. Arlene had already picked out a faux ostrich skin for the cabinets, floor tile recalling fieldstone, and a wall covering aptly called river rock.

It took what seemed to Schriber an inordinately long three months to design the space, but he had never undertaken an entire interior that included all the architectural details, from the flooring to the lighting. Selecting the plumbing fixtures, for example, required hours of research on the web and a day

at a plumbing store with Arlene to find just the right fittings. Most builders have a stock line that they use over and over, but Schriber had never needed plumbing fixtures before so he had to start from scratch.

Picking up on the color of Arlene's faux ostrich, which he used to cover the sides and fronts of the cabinets and the tub surround, Schriber chose lacewood for the wainscot paneling above the sink. The countertop and tub ledge are slate and the sink is patinated zinc. Two sheets of blackened steel wrap around the corner above the vanity to form shelves, and other metal strips serve as dividers between the panels of faux ostrich and lacewood. Schriber describes the rectilinear effect as "Mondrianesque." The other theme in the interior was "things cut into things," like the blackened steel niche for the toilet paper and the switch plate, the notches for the handholds on the vanity, and the fixtures cut into the mirror and the walls above the tub.

"I loved the results and could not have been happier," said Arlene, adding that she was particularly pleased that the project was completed in a timely manner. "James understands a deadline," she said.

Artist: Cameron Van Dyke
Grand Rapids, MI
Client: John Lagrand

Kitchen, 2004, Grand Rapids, MI

Cameron Van Dyke specializes in restoring interiors in the Heritage Hills Historic District of Grand Rapids, which is filled with turn-of-the-twentieth-century homes. He learned his trade after graduating from the Rochester Institute of Technology in the early 1990s when he went to work for furniture maker John Bailey in Lima, New York. There he learned to identify different architectural styles and build cabinets and furniture appropriate to the period.

The Lagrand home was constructed in 1915 using Frank Lloyd Wright plans for a "Fireproof House for $5,000," published in a 1907 issue of the *Ladies' Home Journal*. Although the house had been cut up into three rental units, much of the original interior was intact. The owners had been restoring the house for ten years. The last area was the kitchen. Architect Ed Bolt designed the kitchen space, which was expanded to 500 square feet by combining the original kitchen with the maid's room and bathroom. Grand River Builders made all the exterior and structural changes necessary to accommodate the new space.

Van Dyke then designed, built, finished, and installed all the cabinets, trim, and lighting, and supervised the tile and countertop work. He praises his clients for sparing no expense to do this year-long job correctly. He used more than 2,000 board feet of African mahogany for the cabinets, including a work island and a freestanding dish cupboard. The cabinets conceal a broom closet, roll-out trash cans, pot cupboards, slide-out shelves, and a space for recycling containers. A cantilevered counter at the end of the island provides a place to eat. Held up by two steel beams, the tabletop is strong enough to dance on, Van Dyke says. The bar stools, with no Frank Lloyd Wright precedents, were among the few stock items purchased for the kitchen.

The Mexican tile floor, the crackle gold ceramic tiles on the backsplash of the bar, the leaded glass windows, and even the glass in the cabinet doors all match Wright details found throughout the house. The flat planes of the granite and mahogany countertops, the linear mahogany ceiling beams, and the wide bands circling the tops of the walls all reference the horizontality of Wright's Prairie School architecture. Seven hanging lights, which Van Dyke loosely based on those in Wright's Unity Temple in Oak Park, Illinois, punctuate the space.

Van Dyke's goal was to create a modern kitchen in a historic house while respecting the details and materials used by the original architect. He rightly succeeded.

Faculty Selects 2006

Young makers leap into space

Tim Maddox is working on his thesis pieces in his last semester. I am not insisting on certain assignments but rather helping him find his own voice as he makes the shift from student to professional. To me this chest represents the further beginnings of a merger of his graffiti murals and furniture. With the volume turned up, written text, fonts, funk/soul vibes, early Modern furniture, and the wonderful steel furniture of Jim Rose were all plugged into the building of this piece.

—*Brent Skidmore, instructor*

Nilla Nanna Mix (2007)
Timothy Maddox
Kendall College of Art and Design
of Ferris State University, Grand Rapids, MI
Steel, alder, patina, paint; 36" H x 30" W x 18" D
Photo: Peter McDaniel

The annual Faculty Selects competition is a showcase for student furniture designed and made at the college level. The competition invites each faculty member to nominate an outstanding piece by a student, and to submit up to five images of that piece. A jury then winnowed the entries to what you see on these pages, which this year was about half of the total.

The jury's task was not easy. The primary objective is to show innovative, promising, and well-crafted work, without regard to style. The work can be traditional, contemporary, experimental, or sculptural, though it does need to retain a toehold in the furniture world. Secondary objectives include ensuring broad institutional and geographic representation, avoiding overemphasis on powerhouse schools with many faculty members, and rejecting entries that are photographically inadequate for publication. While this last requirement might seem harsh, jurying from photographs is how things are done in this field, whether for employment, commissions, competitions, exhibitions, or fellowships. Part of being a professional furniture maker is figuring out how to get great photos of your own work.

Notably, only one of the students sent slides, all the others sent digital images. We collected the entries onto CDs with printouts, and distributed them to the jurors for individual review in advance of a telephone-and-computer conference.

College is a heady place where the constraints and opportunities of a well-designed assignment can fuel exuberant leaps into space. If images were all we had, we jurors would have been left gasping. But this competition also requires a written evaluation by the nominating faculty member, giving context and purpose to the work. Without that, remote jurying might be impossible.

In recent years the Faculty Selects competition has included an exhibition at The Furniture Society's annual conference. That was not possible for the 2007 Victoria conference, given the difficulties of cross-border transport. These pages themselves constitute the 2007 exhibition.

The 2006 jury consisted of Dean Wilson, professor at the Minneapolis College of Art and Design, Wayne Raab, woodworking and furniture design instructor at Haywood (NC) Community College, Forest Dickey, a graduate student at San Diego State University who is student representative on The Furniture Society's executive board, plus myself as editor of *Furniture Studio*. Each juror recused himself from discussion of work by his own students, or in Dickey's case, his classmates at SDSU.

—*John Kelsey*

Work that made us say Wow

by Forest Dickey

Every time I go to the library, bookstore, or magazine rack I march, salivating, in search of furniture, sculpture, or products that I consider to be of true originality and technical quality. I comb the vast landscape of publications for a piece that perfectly combines design, craftsmanship, ingenuity, and daring, a piece of furniture that at first glance makes me hold my breath, exhale, and say, "Wow." This initial exclamation is immediately followed by a crushing moment of self-doubt and the reflection, "How can I ever expect to top that?" One can only overcome this doubt by showing the piece to fellow students, thus spreading the sentiment until we return to our benches chastised, heads hung in shame at our inadequacy. Sure, we all say, "Cool," but we are thinking, "Man, I wish I had done that."

This being the case, I think it's an odd contradiction that we students are constantly disappointed when we don't get this feeling from a piece of furniture. Somehow, that moment of red-eared uncertainty is far more stimulating than the humdrum of the everyday. For me, the jurying process included grand moments of disappointment and shame, followed by the bright light of inspiration.

Emotions aside, I believe that this year's Faculty Selects are representative of the great strength and diversity in the studio furniture field. These students and their departments have demonstrated commitment to all facets of our discipline. This work expands our perception and understanding of furniture, while maintaining commitments to technique and craft.

I felt a great privilege at being one of the first individuals from the greater Furniture Society membership to view this year's crop of Faculty Selects. Above all else, the work you see here inspired us to get back to our workspaces to do what we do best: design, make, experiment, and think. It made us all say, "Wow...."

Adirondack Chair (2006)
Michael Floyd
Appalachian Center for Craft,
Tennessee Tech University, Smithville, TN
Walnut veneer, paint on plywood
42" H x 32" W x 48" D
Photo: John Lucas

Students were instructed to design and build a form that would support the human figure in space, using all the technical skills that they knew. Michael Floyd chose to work from a historical source, the Adirondack chair. His resolution took a piece of outdoor furniture for rural second homes and flipped it into an indoor piece for a first house. He accomplished this with clever use of a larger scale and sumptuous surfaces, even though the chair sat in exactly the same way as the original.

—*Graham Campbell, instructor*

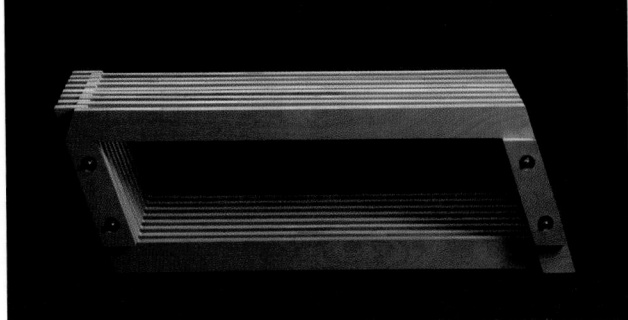

Versatile Coffee Table (2006)
Eric Cole
California Polytechnic State University,
San Luis Obispo
Plywood, threaded rods, washers, bolts
14" H x 44" W x 16" D
Photo: Josef Kasperovich

Eric Cole's table successfully achieved the intent of our school's furniture competition and the assignment for his class. The various forms that his table can take are each beautiful on their own, but that they all can be achieved by quickly moving the two pieces is a testament to its simplicity and ingenuity. Another characteristic that we were looking for was that the piece could be easily reproduced. The table was cut out of two sheets of plywood, something Eric did by hand. But he also had it completely laid out in AutoCAD, so that all the components could be made using a CNC machine.

—*Henri T. de Hahn, department head*

Things happen in the making of an object that are unintended. Sometimes it means starting over, and sometimes, "Whoops, what do I do now?" The last stage of construction involved mounting the top by drilling pilot holes, and needless to say three holes got drilled too deep. Jacque was not appropriating Garry Bennett's signature design statement, but demonstrating the attitude of, "Oh well I goofed, it's only a desk, let's have fun with it and move on." What could have been a devastating mistake served as an opportunity to solve a problem and move the design in a different direction.

—Wayne Raab, instructor

3 Nails and a Desk (2006)
Jacque Allen
Haywood Community College, Clyde, NC
Aluminum, dyed birch plywood, birch top
30" H x 74" W x 21" D
Photo: Jacque Allen

Folded Stool (2006)
Tyler Inman
Rhode Island School of Design, Providence
Birch ply; 20" H x 40" W x 22" D
Photo: Mark Johnston

Tyler Inman's *Folded Stool* is made of 1/8-inch birch plywood, partially routed with V grooves while in a flat panel and laminated to a paper membrane. The form is then folded, creating a structurally sound three-dimensional seating surface. The bottom corners are held together using two friction-fitted copper clips. The *Folded Stool* illustrates design and production principles based on an economy of material usage and is a highly sophisticated yet simple design demonstrating a philosophy of ingenuity and integrity.

—Peter Walker, instructor

(left) *Geisha Display Cabinet* (2006)
Trevor Doig
Selkirk College, Nelson, BC, Canada
Cherry, glass
370mm D x 741mm W x 1760mm H
Photo: Trevor Doig

The project was to construct a cabinet with a door using specified types of joinery in a given time period. The *Geisha* cabinet was an ambitious project. The design was well-resolved, which allowed it to be completed within the time schedule. The piece is quite stunning to look at and is exceptionally well-made.

—*Michael Grace, instructor*

(right) *Mrs. Robinson* (2006)
Edward Ross
Murray State University, Murray, KY
Beech, Spanish cedar, yellow heart
54" H x 22" W x 16" D
Photo: Edward Ross

Ted Ross's current work sprung out of a simple conversation we had about marquetry, parquetry, and inlay. I told him about producing edge banding by sawing, stacking, and gluing different species of wood to make geometric design. Ted, being a curious soul, jumped on this concept and started to produce simple but elegant designs, which he then applied to the surfaces of his furniture. Each late night in the studio brought a new design revelation. Ted's exploration began to have an immediate positive impact in the woodshop, and the other students responded by aggressively using their own but different visual persuasions to produce work. Ted became a catalyst for commitment... what else could an instructor ask for?

—*Paul M. Sasso, professor*

Geoflux 101 (2006)
Robin Bara
Hout en Meubilerings
College, Amsterdam
Ash, steel
55cm x 80cm x 75cm
Photo: John Pompe

The theme Robin Bara chose was 'spring action.' After research on tension and pressure in wood and in possible joints he developed a structure to sit on, a lazy chair or lounge chair combining comfort with clear lines and a simple construction. The user is offered a surprisingly comfortable seating position together with a restricted spring action that makes sitting both relaxing and exciting. The joint below is technically not strong enough for gluing only, so it was reinforced by inserting bent metal rods, and evaluated to comply with the highest level back and seat fatigue test. We consider his result a successful combination of sound technical execution and a design that is both innovative and embedded in tradition.

—*Jan Leijtens and Erik Groenhout, senior teachers*

Bench for Linens (2006)
Nate Blaisdell
School for American Crafts,
Rochester (NY) Institute of Technology
Hard maple, micro-suede,
milk paint, brushed nickel
48" L x 17" W x 18" H
Photo: RIT Staff

This piece has a bench top that hinges open to access an interior storage area. The faculty was impressed by its elegant line quality and sensitivity to negative space. With cutaways revealing the interior space and subtle milk paint accents, this piece brings together good craftsmanship, traditional joinery, and structural details that enhance the form and functional identity.

—*Rich Tannen and Andy Buck, instructors*

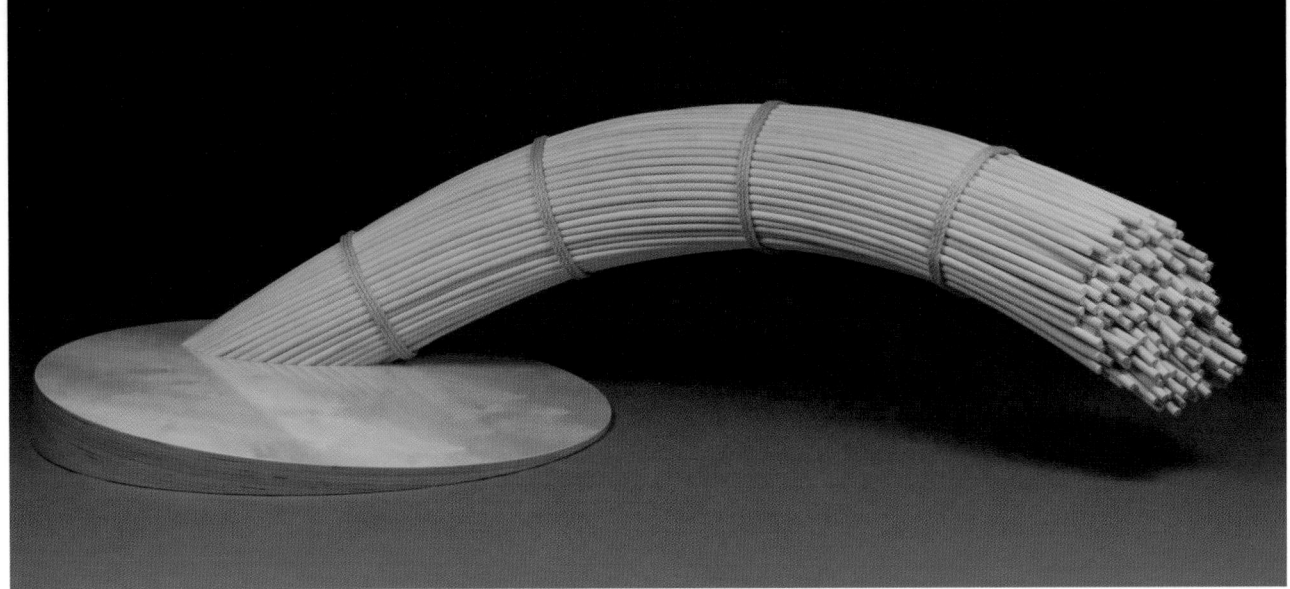

Over the Rainbow (2006)
Myoungtaek Jung
School for American Crafts,
Rochester (NY)
Institute of Technology
Rattan, rope, maple, plywood, steel
120" L x 50" W x 36" H
Photo: RIT staff

...the first in a series of seating pieces created as part of Myoungtaek Jung's thesis investigation. His goals were to investigate public seating and the ways in which it might stimulate interaction, or communication, among those using the piece. While agreeing that it was a fascinating, strong object, Myoungtaek and his thesis committee members engaged in lively debate as to how well the piece addressed the utilitarian issue of seating. The healthy debate continues!

—Rich Tannen and Andy Buck, instructors

The assignment was to design and build a cabinet or other case piece using solid timber.... Mifflin transformed his case piece into a table. Mitered boxes extend off a central box that has a sliding glass door on top, to present drawers at each end. Of particular interest are the friction-fit, cantilevered legs that easily can be placed anywhere along the form... a fully realized functional object that is satisfying in scale and proportion and has an enhanced interactive quality through the adjustability of the legs. This deceptively simple table could be re-examined, via sheet materials, for production.

—David Upfill-Brown, instructor

Five Boxes (2005)
T. J. Mifflin
Center for Furniture
Craftsmanship, Rockville, ME
Hard maple, walnut, glass
16" H x 56" W x 20" D
Photo: Jim Dugan

Chair (2006)
Tristan Thiel
Minneapolis (MN) College
of Art and Design
Stainless steel, leather
30" H x 27" W x 36" D
Photo: Tristan Thiel

This assignment was to design and fabricate a piece of metal furniture with no welding for its structure. Tristan Thiel's chair is fabricated from stainless steel bar and plate, using flat-head socket-cap screws as fasteners, giving the frame the look of a bridge with rivets. Standing in contrast to that industrial look are soft, smooth leather cushions sewed in a traditional manner. Ergonomic concerns, design parameters, and finish details were worked out in detailed drawings, yielding excellent results.

—Dean Wilson, professor

KA (the Slash) (2006)
Chung Shen (Johnson) Tang
California Polytechnic State University, San Luis Obispo
Corrugated cardboard, glue
20" H x 32" W x 28" D
Photo: Chung Shen Tang and Michelle Chan

Chung Shen Tang set out to create an honest, reproducible, lightweight, 'switch rich,' yet affordable piece of furniture that could be adapted to a stool, chair, chaise longue, various tables, storage device, candleholder, and/or bookshelf… all from a modest amount of cardboard and glue. Very economical. He wanted it to be simple, compact, flexible, expandable, and portable. He triumphed on every level.

—Henri T. de Hahn, department head

Eren Ulsever's furniture exhibits a high level of consideration of the challenges and limitations of living in small spaces. We view furniture as tools for living and Eren has expressed this in a very tangible way…. The leaning wall unit is truly responsive to the needs of the user, with its removable, upholstered backrest cushions, pop-out plastic shelves, and mobile sofa/bed/storage combination. The welded aluminum tables with cushions serve as armrests when mated to the sofa as well as stools and docking for a lap desk (not shown). He has sensitively and successfully combined natural and manmade materials into a collection of furniture that is warm, visually engaging, functional, and responsive to the needs of his audience.

—*George Perez, instructor*

Incode (2006)
Eren Ulsever
Savannah (GA) College of Art and Design
Ash, plastic, aluminum, upholstry
78" H x 82" W x 45" D

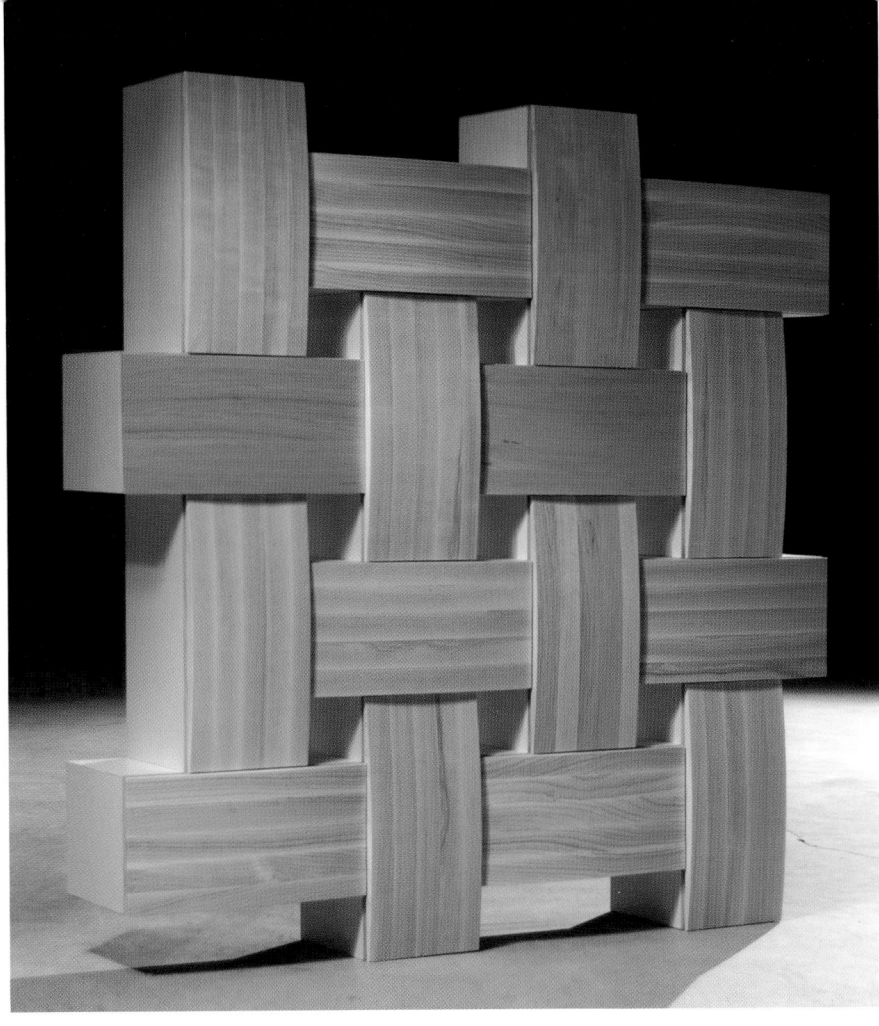

Woven Cabinet (2006)
Leslie Webb
Sheridan College, Toronto,
ON, Canada
White ash, solid and veneer
48" H x 48" W x 8.5" D
Photo: Leslie Webb

Leslie Webb designed and made this cabinet in her second year as the major project for one semester. It is a remarkable exploration of form, its simplicity of concept belying the complexity of planning and fabrication. It is flawlessly executed using traditional furniture techniques. The piece stands 48 inches high, and may be used as a room divider or against a wall. The choice of quarter-sawn ash for all elements was particularly appropriate, lending a linear element to the composition, which is an investigation in light, shadow, volume, and mass.

—*Peter Fleming, studio head*

Deformation (2006)
Adam Tolsma
Minneapolis (MN)
College of Art and Design
Glass, PVC, vinyl, ebony, stainless steel
27" W x 27" D x 17" H
Photo: Adam Tolsma

...one result of several exercises to design a flat-pack production table that Adam Tolsma did for an advanced furniture class. One goal was a short set-up time using minimum tools. This was achieved using screws, clips, and standoffs to assemble four identical pieces of PVC in minutes, with only a screwdriver. A successful blend of form, structure, and utility.

—*Dean Wilson, professor*

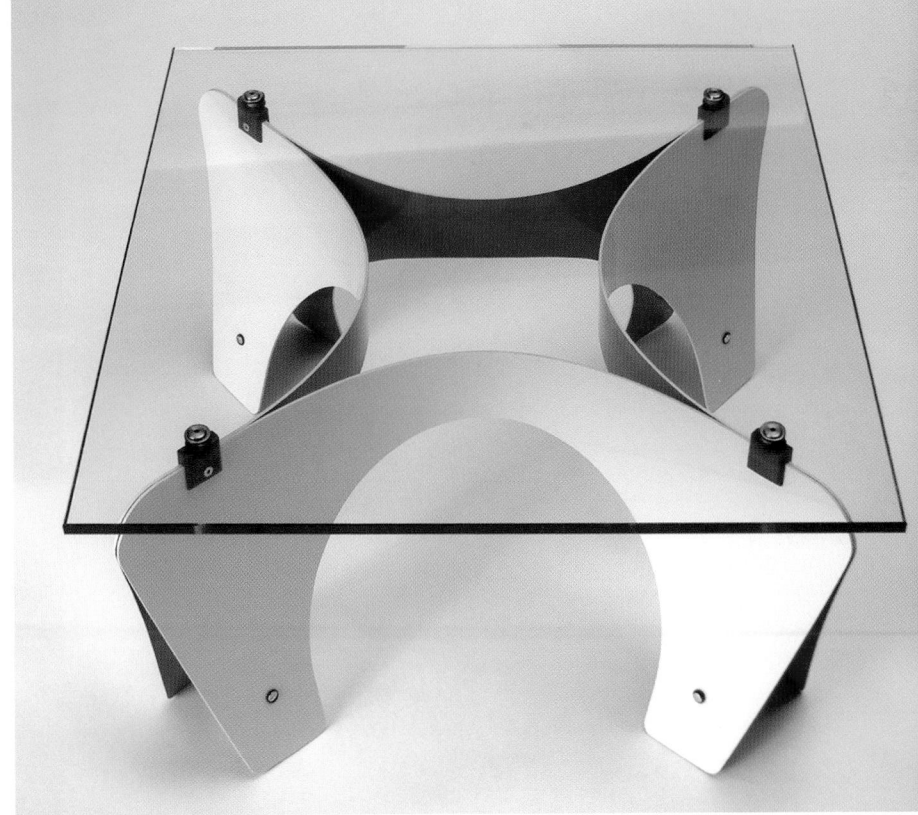

Table (2005)
George Dubinsky
Rhode Island School of Design, Providence
Cherry
22" H x 18" W x 13" D
Photo: Mark Johnston

…the final assignment in the first semester sophomore design. The requirements of the project are to design and build a small table in hardwoods using primarily hand tools. The requirements include limiting the number of parts, using hand-cut mortise and tenon joints, and hand-planed surfaces. Dubinski exceeded all requirements, creating an elegant table that is well-resolved both conceptually and formally, has great attention to subtle details of shaping, color, and joinery, and is very approachable.

—*John Dunnigan, professor*

Plant Stand (2006)
Ward Stevens
Bucks County
Community College,
Newtown, PA
Beech, birch, paint
37" H x 18.5" W x 18.5" D
Photo: John Carlano

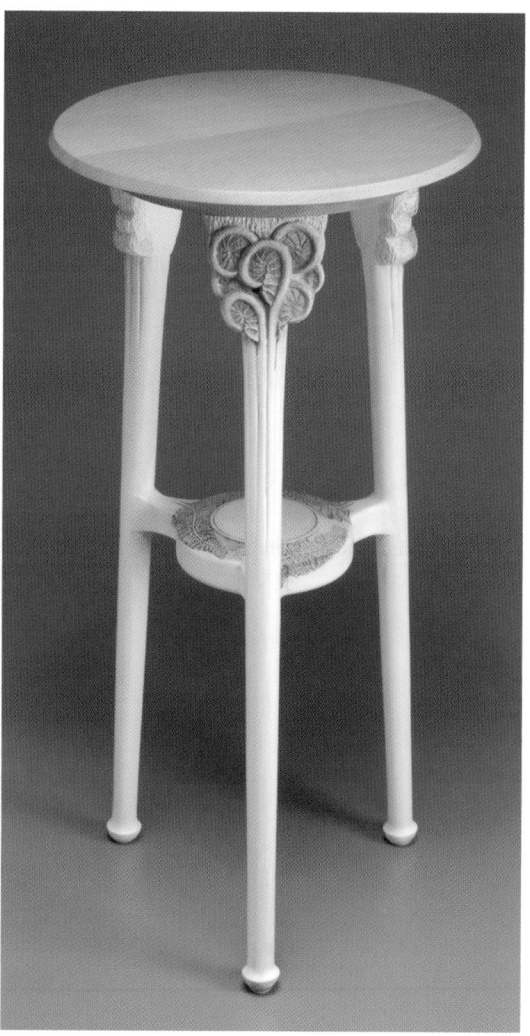

Second-semester students are required to make a table of their own design. Ward Stevens took on a project that involved turning, shaping, and bas-relief carving, plus the use of color. He was thorough in working out the carving details by making a full-sized mockup in poplar and even carving a sample corner. His contrast of the pristine turned natural wood top works well against the more organic base structure. The carving is skillful and the way he chose to have the carved detailing fade away is very well done.

—*Mark Sfirri, professor*

The Dowry Project, from Harrington's MFA research, involves multiple versions, mutations, and morphings of an iconic Hadley dowry chest in the collection of the Milwaukee Museum. Harrington's first reinterpretation is an impeccably crafted version that uses precise reconstructions of the joinery but leaves out the panels, allowing complete access to what usually is a very private space. Other versions explored what happens with a change of materials, the use of metaphorical surface ornament, or the merging of furniture types. The final installation (not shown) involved many chests stacked on top of each other, as well as an architectural construction that both sheltered and made inaccessible the dowry chest inside.... I admire this work because of its visual beauty as an installation. I also appreciate Harrington's careful framing of the conceptual issues, and I love her thoughtful and thorough exploration of materials and techniques....

—Tom Loeser, instructor

Dowry (2006) with Dowager #1 (2005)
B. A. Harrington
University of Wisconsin–Madison
Dowry: 9'2" H x 11' W x 4'10" D;
Dowager #1: 36" H x 45" W x 20" D
Dowry: 2x4s, 2x8s, 2x10s, #8 and #16 nails;
Dowager #1: quartersawn red oak, aniline dye,
linseed oil, brass hinges
Photo: Stephen Funk

Bernie and Phyl (2006)
Chris Todd
University of Massachusetts–Dartmouth
Basswood
20" D x 33" W x 70" H
Photo: Chris Todd

Chris Todd's unusual chairs do function, but not in the traditional ways that chairs serve their users. The utility of these chairs is embedded in the metaphors they create—their use by the viewer is an imaginary bridge into the emotional states of the artist and our own psychological walkabouts. Built with figurative animation and gesture, the chairs threaten to come to life, but more importantly they speak of the evolution of the spirit, the mastering of one's self and one's environment. Chris unsettles our expectations for the 'normal,' but her careful resolve of form leaves us with a feeling that the spirit will triumph over fears and doubts.

—*Stephen Whittlesey, instructor*

(right) Accoutrements from the Planet Zoron (2006)
Brad Johns
San Diego State University, CA
Wood, acrylic, aluminum
Photo: Larry Stanley

In this day and age of new advances in CNC technology and CAD/CAM software, the work of Brad Johns brings us a nostalgic view of the marvels of machines as seen through the eyes of a child. A child viewing toys that employed cranks, gears, whirlygigs, and bright colors for the first time evokes that sense of glee and wonder.

—*Wendy Maruyama, professor*

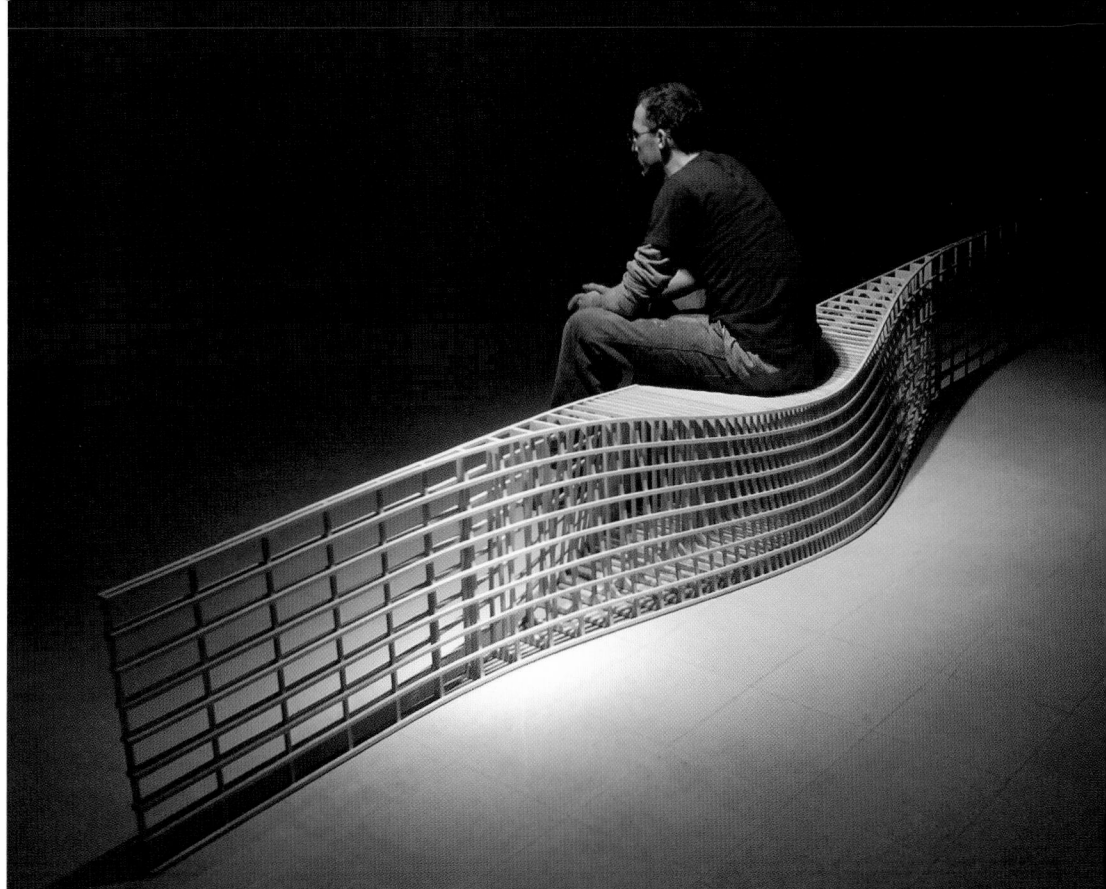

Deviated Path (2006)
Matthew Pliessnig
University of
Wisconsin–Madison
Ash
168" W x 27" D x 23" H
Photo:
Matthias Pliessnig

This bench form is the result of a successful blend of meticulous pre-planning followed by a more spontaneous building process: the initial idea was generated by bending a dollar bill and manipulating the flat paper into a three-dimensional form, developed with freehand sketches, many models, and many 3D renderings.... The finished piece is a visual knockout. Much of the structural interest comes from repetition and visual progression.... Every time I look at the piece I am intrigued by a different area. It varies tremendously as one walks around it. Pleissnig's *Deviated Path* is a powerful blend of a simple form and a complex structure that offers a rewarding sitting experience and a challenging visual event."

—*Tom Loeser, instructor*

Peg Bench (2006)
Christina Boy
VirginiaCommonwealthUniversity, Richmond
Soft maple, milk paint, walnut
48" W x 13" D x 17" H
Photo: Christina Boy

This was Tina's solution to the bench assignment. It certainly references what might be the center or mainstream in studio furniture. It has nice presence and form, is whimsical and playful, and is well-crafted to carry out the idea.

—*William Hammersley*

Tommy Simpson

"I was an artist whether I liked it or not. It's what flows best in me."

introduction by Jonathan Binzen,
photo captions by Tommy Simpson with Jonathan Binzen

In a career that now spans more than 40 years, Tommy Simpson has produced a shipload of interesting furniture. But that doesn't make him a furniture maker. To Simpson, furniture is just one means of expression among many. A graduate of the Cranbrook Academy of Art, Simpson is as productive in painting and sculpture as in furniture. Other avenues for his creativity include printmaking, drawing, and jewelry making. He also likes making toys, and produces custom cookie cutters for special occasions. And over the last decade he has been designing one-of-a-kind rugs to be hand-knotted in Nepal. The various outlets for his artistry are all related, he finds. Ideas that arise while making jewelry might well find their expression in furniture. "It's all composition," he says, "whatever the medium."

Simpson was born in 1939 and grew up in the small town of Dundee, Illinois. It was a farming area, and Simpson learned the rudiments of woodworking from local farmers. Simpson's furniture, especially, is rich with imagery and carved text that evokes his Midwestern upbringing. "I loved the simple, straightforward, can-do approach of the world I grew up in," he says. And although some of the people he grew up around might be surprised by the

Tommy Simpson displays the Gord Peteran sculpture presented to him at The Furniture Society's 2006 conference in Indianapolis. Photo: John Kelsey.

irony and abstraction in some of his furniture, they would certainly identify with the speed and resourcefulness with which it is made.

Simpson grew up in a family of doctors and everyone expected he would become one too. But at the end of his first semester of pre-med studies in college he turned in all his exams blank and took a tramp steamer to Hawaii. When he returned he studied business, but after a couple of electives in art it began to dawn on him that "I was an artist whether I liked it or not. It's what flows best in me."

What flows through all Simpson's work in every medium is a pure boyish élan—zest, humor, joy, irony, fun. In his book *Two Looks to Home* (oh, yes, he writes books, too), after comparing the creative impulse to a sweet tooth, he writes, "It's that addictive lusciousness of just being alive in the release of self-consciousness that is so bewitching, so seductive, so sweet."

Simpson received the Furniture Society's Award of Distinction in June 2006, presented during the Society conference at the Herron School of Art and Design in Indianapolis. His book, *Two Looks to Home: The Art of Tommy Simpson*, was published by Bullfinch Press in 1999. He is also the coauthor, with Lisa Hammel and William Bennett Seitz, of *Hand and Home: Inside the Homes of American Craftsmen*, and of the seminal classic *Fantasy Furniture: Design and Decoration*, published by Reinhold in 1968, both now out of print.

Simpson family home (1939)

I grew up in this house, in Dundee, Illinois, where five generations of my mother's family lived. There was a tin bathtub upstairs and in the bedroom closets you could find beaver hats and the kind of waistcoats Lincoln wore. My mother's mother was raised in this house. The man she married grew up in the house diagonally across the intersection. When they got married they built a house on the third corner. My father was a doctor, and so was his father. I thought I would go into medicine too, but in college I took an art class and before long I realized that's where my heart was. I've been an artist ever since.

Tommy Simpson (1942). Bang.

Bedroom, Simpson House
(bed 1980, bedroom 1983)

Once in a while I let the wood suggest the shape of a piece. This bed is made from slabs of English brown oak that I bought from an old cabinet shop. They had a stack of boards that had been lying there since the shop bought them in 1932. The owner asked if I was interested and I said I didn't think I could afford them. Two weeks later when I returned to the shop the owner said, "You still interested in that English oak? Fifty bucks for the lot." So I took it all.

Rubber Stamp Self-Portrait (1999)

I drew this self-portrait and had it made into a rubber stamp to use on envelopes. When I went to pick up my order, the guy at the shop looked at the stamp, then looked at me and asked if I was going into politics. Interesting question.

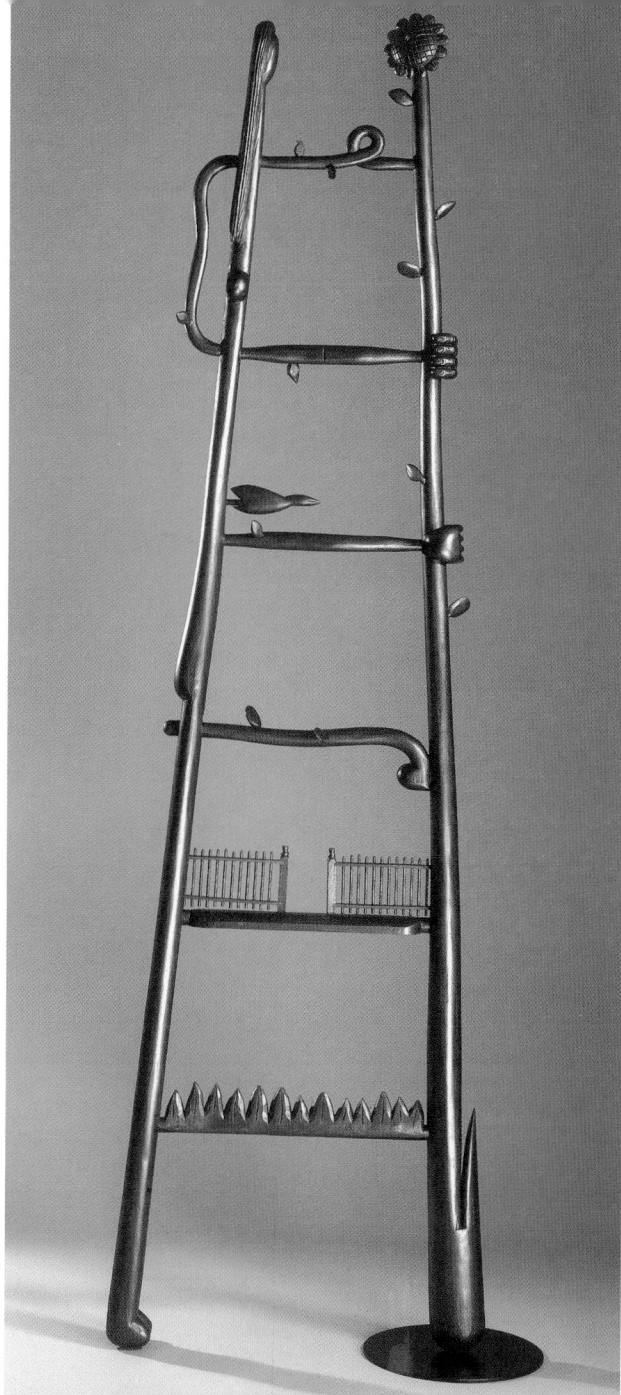

Shadows in Bloom (1997)
Wood, graphite paint
85" H x 24" W x 4" D

I've created a number of pieces in a ladder form like this. The openings in the ladder give me the opportunity to create a series of pictures. These open spaces can form something of a narrative. For this particular ladder I wanted the feeling of midnight in a moonlit garden. So I finished it with graphite paint and polished the surface to simulate nighttime reflections.

Writer's Cabinet (1985)
Mixed woods, glass, zinc
78" H x 36" W x 18" D

On occasion commissions come my way. For example, I built this cabinet for a book dealer to hold his personal collection of rare books. On the pediment I carved a pair of scribes and a quill pen, and on the lower door panels I carved the names of some of the client's favorite authors and musicians. Etched in the glass panels there is a rabbit, after John Updike's Rabbit Angstrom, and a frog for Mark Twain's *The Celebrated Jumping Frog of Calaveras County*. The drawer pulls are beer taps—because the client mentioned a quote about most writers getting their inspiration from the keg. And the pun on the 2B pencils, that's Shakespeare, of course.

Two People Carrying Their Sex Around (1968)
Wood, paint
62" H x 48" W x 24" D

These days I am interested in simple forms of Early American furniture. But many of my pieces, like this table from the sixties, are much more sculptural, more like *Alice In Wonderland* themes—they're the kind of thing none of us have ever seen before. They deal with forms that are literary or pictorial rather than related to Western classical furniture. But whether I am working in a classical or personal form I try to bring my own voice to the artwork. After all, instilling one's artwork with personal vocabulary is a lot more individual in its expression, be it a small element found in a classical shape, or pure creative fantasy. This personal vocabulary is harder for people to grasp, but it can be a lot more rewarding for both the artist and viewer.

Sawhorse (1989)
Mixed woods
30" H x 18" W x12" D

Years ago I needed sawhorses, so I made a pair. I enjoyed working with the idea so much that I've made them ever since. Some are 30 inches high and several times people have bought a pair and made a table by putting a glass top on them. Other people have used them as quilt stands, folding and hanging the quilt like a saddle blanket.

My Mummy Made Me Do It (1982)
Wood, cotton fabric
43" H x 26" W x 38" D

A lot of craft schools give students weeks or months to build one piece of furniture.
I think it's important not to belabor the task. I believe a timely execution keeps the idea
fresh. I made this chair in two days while I was teaching a workshop. I screwed the rocker
together instead of making mortises and tenons, and for a finish I wrapped the chair with
cotton rug strips. But speed wasn't the lesson plan, keeping the idea playful and genuine
was more the point.

(below) G.W. Cabinet (1994)
Wood, paint, copper leaf
76" H x 32" W x 19" D
Renwick Collection

If you go antiquing in the Pennsylvania German country you'll come across little papiér mâché holiday candy containers called whimsies. They were made for children of all ages. The inspiration for this cabinet was seeing a whimsy celebrating George Washington's birthday in the shape of a stump with a hatchet in it. I built the piece with stave construction, like a barrel, and gave it a faux finish with a wood-graining tool. I made the hatchet out of poplar and copper-leafed the blade.

(above) The Night Feather Tickles My Still (1993)
Mixed woods, wrought iron
45" H x 34" W x 28" D

I usually make a chair in two weeks. Working quickly is essential to getting myself into the spirit of spontaneity and to keeping myself interested. If a piece takes too long to make I may bog down and never finish. So I try not to let the creative process take too long.

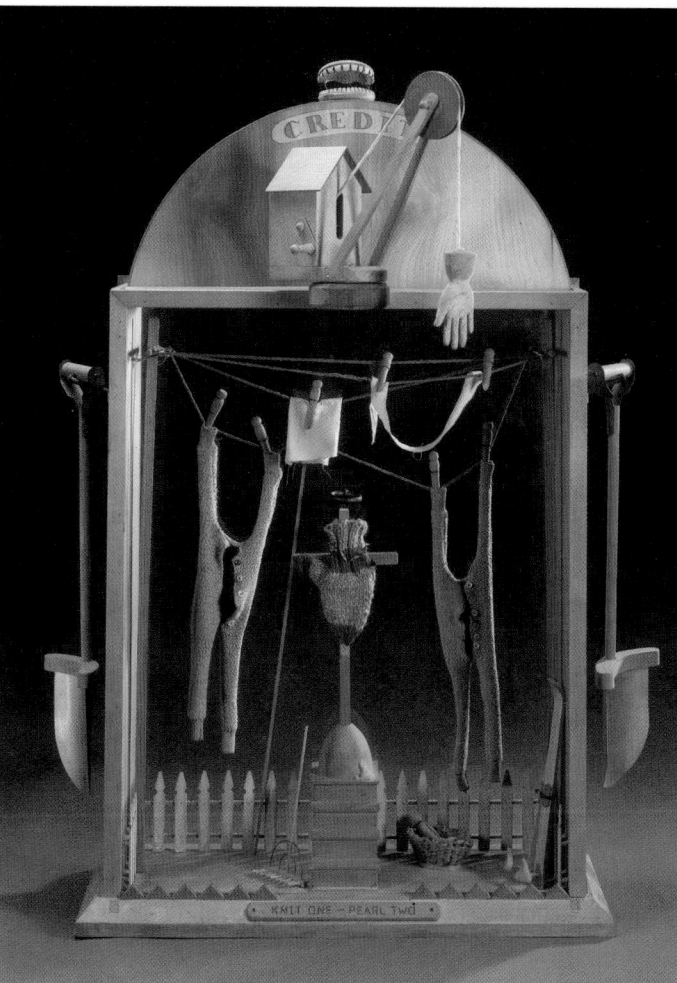

Toys (1986)
Mixed media

Sometimes I make little toys for fun. It has to be for fun, because you can't charge enough to pay for the time it takes to make them. It's a little like writing a haiku—the form may be short, but if you want to get it right, it could take you as long as writing an epic poem. I was thinking of my mother when I made the pogo-crucifix. When she came upon us kids "up to something" she'd say, "Good God, what are you doing now?"

Knit One, Pearl Two (1984)
Wood, metal, fabric,
knitted mitten
40" H x 28" W x 9" D

In this piece I was spoofing on the Ashcan School—the early 20th century artists in New York who found significance in poor urban scenes. So I've got a humble garden scene with a mitten being crucified between two criminals being hung out to dry. Why a mitten? It's such an innocent thing—can you think of anything bad about a mitten? This piece also has some elements from medieval religious art, like the hand of God descending from above, and shovels hanging nearby, which symbolize the resurrection.

Carpenter's Chair (1991)
Mixed woods and media
56" H x 36" W x 24" D

This particular chair is a narrative homage to the Shakers. I often use the Windsor
chair as an expressive medium because I tend to solve compositions in a linear
manner and Windsor chairs, with all their small parts, lend themselves to this
process. When I use unpainted classical forms like this, I work within those elements.
In other words, I riff off of an established idea. Then the story or the creative narrative
within the piece can begin.

Adobe Domus (1992)
Wood, paint
67" H x 64" W x 84" D

When I make a piece like this that has carved, painted panels, I make the complete bed first. Then I draw directly on the wood. Next I carve and paint it. As I carve I change the drawing, depending on what seems to work, or not. I work this way because drawings in a sketchbook often take on a different relationship when blown up to a larger scale. Once the bed is carved to my satisfaction then I undercoat with gesso. Next I'll paint the whole thing with color five or six times, changing parts of the composition each time. It's like a garden—you plant the first year and wait to see what you like and what you don't. After a number of seasons you have a good garden.

Kilua (2002)
Knotted wool
7' L x 5' W

The rug *Kilua* was inspired by the time I lived in Hawaii when I was 17—homage to the impressions of a Midwestern boy who encounters the ocean for the first time. About ten years ago I started designing rugs. I begin with a gouache painting and then I have the design made into a hand-knotted, one-of-a-kind rug in Kathmandu, Nepal. I've discovered that for a lot of people, it's easier to approach something that functions. Somebody might see a painting on the wall and feel intimidated by what they perceive as precious artwork. But if they see the same image in a rug, they instantly take to it.

Tooling Tennessee Box (1994)
Basswood, iron, acrylic
18" H x 24" W x 10" D

I built this toolbox while I was teaching a workshop in Tennessee. It gave students an opportunity to see the way I work, and it kept me out of trouble for the week. I made the box, then drew on it with a pencil. Next I carved and painted the surface. And then I glued in a fringe of brush bristles at either end of the closure. Visually, the brushes are a decorative molding, but they also function as a structural element to keep the lid in place until you pull it open.

Red Horse (1993)
Pastel
22" H x 32" W

I love to paint, draw, make furniture, make sculpture, toys, jewelry... work in any number of different mediums. Each has its particular characteristics—painting is more esoteric, for example, more in the head, and furniture making is more physical—but in essence they're all the same. I go from one medium to another as ideas and emotions dictate; I try not to over-think the process. I just create.

Workspace with Tommy Horizontal (1998)

I call the place where I work "my space" rather than my studio or shop.
But inside the artist's world the creative space needs no definition, it's just me.

Sketchbook (1990s)

I always have a sketchbook nearby,
and I'll pick it up whenever I have an
idea—or when I'm looking for one.
I usually carry a little pad with me
when I go to museums. I'm always
searching for new design solutions,
and I'll find things here and there.
It might be a motif in a Botticelli or
a Matisse painting. This process of
discovery is a little like a writer riding
on a bus. You know, when somebody
three seats up says something that
catches your attention and you think,
Gee, that's a good phrase, so you jot
it down.

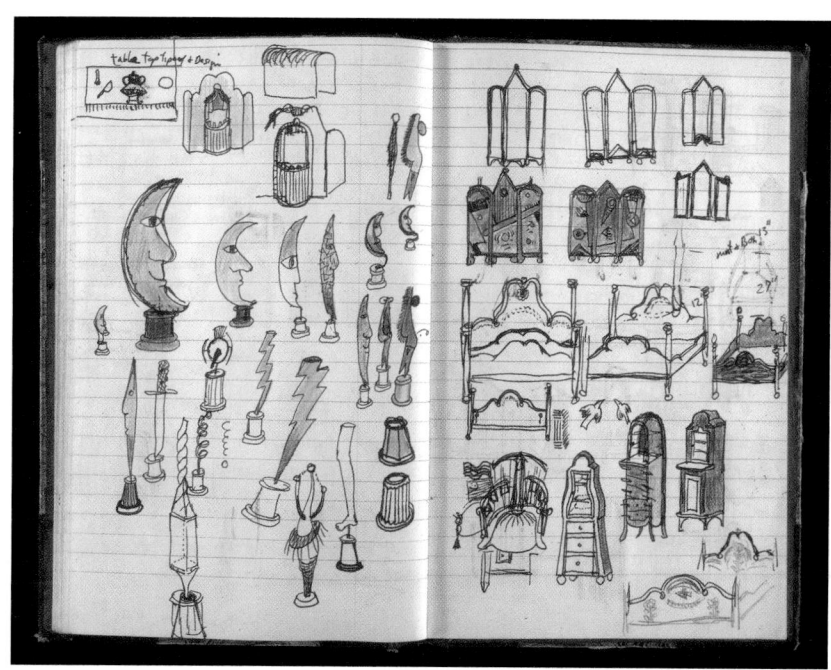

Photos by: William Seitz, Bibiana Matheis, Garry Burdick, John Kane,
Sally Anderson Bruce, David Caras, Michael Meken, Gretchen Tatge,
Tom Kneebone, Brad Stanton, Karen LaFleur.

An American Benchmaker in Paris: Vive la Différence!

by Mitch Ryerson

On a trip I made to France a couple of years ago I noticed what appeared to be a very different attitude toward public seating from the one I was accustomed to in the United States. I decided to do some research about this topic and, if possible, to return and study it in a more organized fashion. Thanks to an education grant I received from The Furniture Society, I was able to return to Paris last spring to photograph many benches and to meet with several people there who are involved with public seating in the city. The results of my research are not in any way comprehensive or objective. I have simply compiled my own personal responses to what I observed and tried to present them here along with a few of the pictures I took.

Paris is, of course, famous for its parks and gardens. It is known as "the capitol of 400 gardens" although in fact there are many more than this.[1] It is a city that seems to live through its public spaces, both physically and culturally. The giant old parks on the east and west sides of the city, Le Bois de Vincennes and Le Bois de Boulogne, are referred to as the "green lungs" of the city. The river Seine runs between them, injecting life and space into this densely populated place. Spread throughout the city, the myriad of parks, large and small, ancient and modern, are the focal points of their neighborhoods, open spaces that provide room for people and plants to flourish.

"A park without a bench is not a park!" So says an official of the city's department responsible for the management of the public parks.[2] This seems like a simple statement, but it is one that has not been understood in its most basic sense in many American cities. Often benches here are regarded suspiciously, viewed as invitations to the homeless, to teenage gangs, to social predators. By removing or limiting them it is possible to keep the parks looking more presentable for the simple reason that they are less lived in. Although this is undoubtedly an issue for the parks in Paris as well, as an outsider looking in it seems that there is a much greater awareness and commitment to the importance of making people feel welcome and comfortable in their public spaces. People in Paris do seem to live in their public spaces on a scale that is not seen in the U.S. There are countless examples of this difference: the groups of old men playing boules, the innumerable outdoor markets, the rows of ladies chatting on the benches, the lovers oblivious to the world, the thousands of cafés with tables and chairs on the street, the many playgrounds that are thronged with parents and children. These things happen everywhere of course, but here there is the sense that they are actively supported and encouraged. Huge new parks have been created in the last twenty years right in the city, with no expense spared. This is not considered a frivolous waste of money, but a logical continuation of the evolution, which began in earnest in the mid-19th century, of the city as a public place. There is also a

strong movement led by community groups to take vacant lands, such as abandoned railway lines, and transform them from neglected, dangerous places to thriving neighborhood centers for teaching, growing, and relaxing.[3]

Bois de Boulogne, 19th Century
This large circular bench features a cast-iron frame with wood slats for the seat and back.

Modern cities are centers of a seated culture.[4] To understand this it is helpful to imagine a kind of typology of public seating that separates it into three main categories: moving seating, seating for waiting, and seating for resting. Each category has its own requirements, although there is some overlap as well (wheelchairs for example). Moving seating includes trains, buses, taxis, cars, etc. Seating for waiting includes train stations, bus stops, airports, etc. Seating for resting is really just parks and the larger avenues. In a world that is becoming more and more dominated by the mentality of "hurry up and wait," the first two categories of seating sometimes seem on the verge of obliterating the third. The idea of sitting somewhere and doing absolutely nothing is frowned upon. Yet a bench in a park is more than just a place to rest your tired legs. It is a place to make unexpected as well as expected encounters.

(facing page) Canal St. Martin, 19th Century. Along the canals and avenues people sit on all sorts of things. On the left are typical "banc double" designed by A. Alphand with the classic tree and lamp accompaniment.

It is a place where people become the glue that can hold a community together.

In the 1970s the American urban planner W. H. Whyte studied many public spaces that either did or did not serve their purpose well. He determined that one of the key ingredients to a successful space was the presence of public seating. People would use a place that welcomed them. His phrase was "sociability attracts sociability."[5] Paris seems quite comfortable with this idea. Much of the seating in the city is carefully arranged in groups of several benches or chairs together. Although chairs are inherently less sociable than benches, their use in several of the newer parks (Villette, Bercy) is

clearly designed to encourage people to interact with each other. This re-introduction of chairs as public seating is interesting when considered in the context of the perennial struggle between private versus public use of open space. In 17th century Paris, before the commitment to parks for all the citizens was made, there were "chaisieres," whose occupation was renting chairs to the upper classes as they strolled along the avenues. Although these chair renters resisted vigorously, they were eventually put out of business by the creation of free public seating.

The "banc double," or back-to-back bench, is an iconic image of Paris. It is used in great numbers

(top left) Montmartre tramway, 20th Century. On the highest hill in the city, this very modern glass tramway booth looks out over some of the oldest neighborhoods in Paris.

(above) The 19th Century banc double is found throughout the city and takes many forms.

(left) Square du Vert Gallant, 19th Century. Large circular bench in a rustic style uses pre-cast concrete.

along the avenues and in the more formal parks. It is particularly appropriate for long rows of benches alternating with trees and punctuated with lamposts. This three-part formula was first developed by the landscape architect Alphand in the 19th century, when the city was being rebuilt on a grand scale.[6] The banc double allows for many kinds of social interactions. This flexibility is an essential quality for good public seating that is often ignored nowadays. The decision to divide a bench with armrests is an example of this new, fundamentally anti-social approach. By restricting the benches, armrests prevent a variety of ways to use the seat. In Paris I saw many people enjoying a comfortable lying-down nap in the sunshine.

This activity seemed to be totally acceptable, yet it is deliberately made impossible by many of the designs currently used in the United States.

In addition, there are many places to sit in the city that are not really defined at all. Low walls, steps, and embankments are incorporated into many of the new public spaces, almost like benches in disguise. These answer the evolving needs of large groups to gather together after the older, more formal parks have been locked up for the night. These gatherings, as well the crowded cafés on the streets and the bustling markets, make it clear that people in Paris are more comfortable being near each other than people in the U.S. are, and the way

(above) Paris Metro, 21st Century. An example of seating-for-waiting, this is one variation of the leaning benches found throughout the Paris subway system.

(left) Parc André-Citroën, Paris 1992. This very modern 34-acre park was created on the site of the former car factory. These stainless steel and teak benches reflect a theme seen throughout the park of combining high-tech and organic forms.

they use benches and public spaces seems much less self-conscious.[7] Perhaps the great variety of seating and its availability reinforces this.

The one thing that seems to be less common are one-of-a-kind benches produced by their designers for a specific place. Where I live, in Cambridge, Massachusetts, there are several successful examples of this more American approach. Bill Keyser's huge stack-laminated bench at the Alewife train station, and Judy McKie's bronze cats at the Valente Library Reading Garden, are two that come to mind. I did see a few benches in Paris that were truly individual sculptures,[8] but for the most part they were either very traditional or were quite high-tech industrial design.

The challenge to provide public seating that meets the needs of a greater and greater variety of situations certainly requires a great variety of approaches. It seemed to me that Paris is addressing this challenge with energy and determination. With its long tradition of urban planning and landscape design to draw upon, the city continues to invite people to come outside, to walk, to play, to visit, and not least of all, to sit down.

Notes

1. Jarrassé, Dominique, *L'Art des Jardins Parisiens,* (Paris: Parigramme, 2002).

2. Jolé, Michele, "Quand la ville s'invite à s'asseoir," *Les Annals de la Recherche Urbaine,* number 94.

3. A good example of this is Les Jardins du Ruisseau in the 18th arrondissement.

4. Jolé, Michele, "Les Assis," *Urbanisme,* number 325 (2002).

5. Whyte, W. H., *The Social Life of Small Urban Places,* The Conservation Foundation (1980).

6. Alphand, A., *Les promenades de Paris,* 2 vol., (Paris: Rothschild, 1867–1873).

7. To get the idea of this, listen to the song by Georges Brassens "Les amoureux qui becotte sur les bancs public."

8. Boursier-Mougenot, E., *L'Amour du Banc,* (Arles: Actes Sud, 2002).

(above) Mitch Ryerson
Fresh Pond Wave Bench
Cambridge, MA, 2005
20" H x 84" L x 31" D

(top) Mitch Ryerson
Little Fresh Pond Bench
Cambridge, MA, 2006
Ipé, steel, stone
39" H x 300" L x 48" D

Index